GRIEF, JOY & ART

GRIEF, JOY & ART

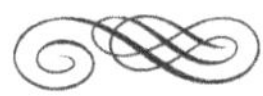

*A True Story
of Love*

SARA JOSEPH

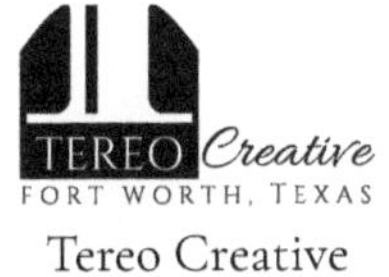

Tereo Creative

Contents

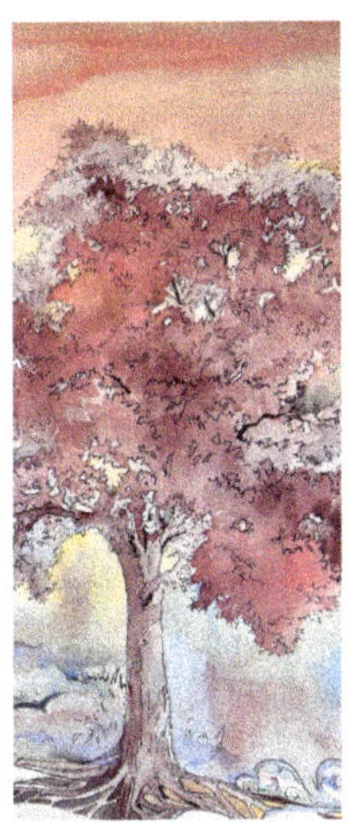

Dedicated to Jesus,
Redeemer
of
the darkest seasons
of human experience.
His compassion is matchless.

I

Preface

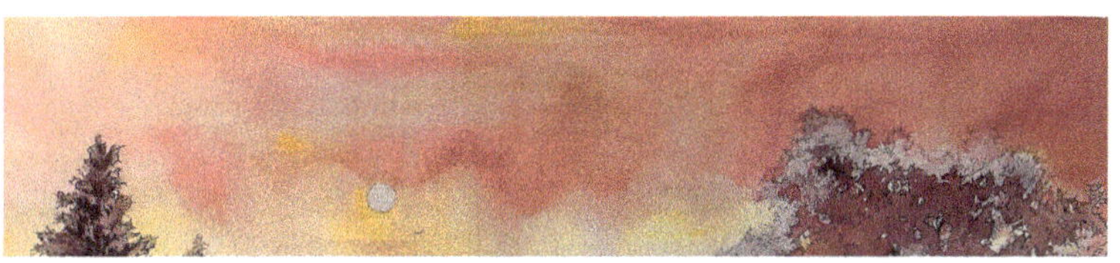

> *"The path of the just is as the shining light,*
> *that shineth more and more unto the perfect day."*
> Proverbs 4:18 KJV

Faint blush of salmon stains the sky
Inky night bids a swift goodbye
Color spilled, relentless flow
The dawn of day a forceful glow
No man can bottle this fuchsia hue
Day once begun will stride on through
Dimming darkness and gaining strength
The day must live its destined length

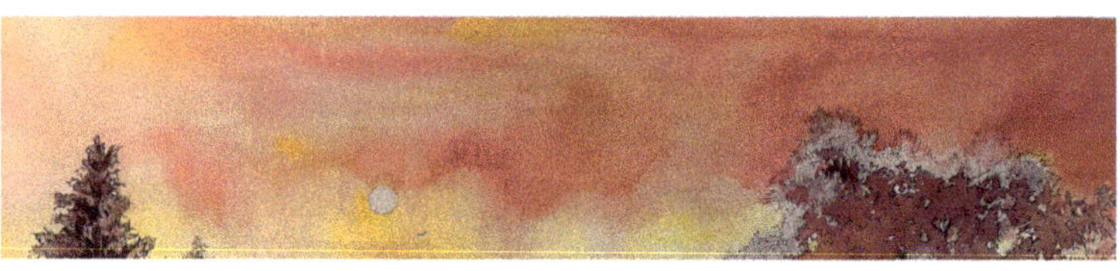

Quiet whisper bids me learn
A lesson from the gleam of dawn.
" You walk a path, Oh Righteous One,
Which like first radiant beam of sun
Dispels darkness and welcomes Me
Though faint at first, with little to see
Shining brighter till full force of day
Destined for glory though fashioned of clay."

What joy to know that once begun
No turning back the blazing sun
My way will march the way of dawn
Until my time on earth is done

Brighter, sharper, erasing night
No taint of ink, no dimming sight
From glory to glory ever bold
From blush to fuchsia and then to gold.

2

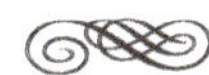

Death, Where is Your Sting?

This is a love story.

But if you expect to settle into your favorite chair, sighing at the thought of reading about the fragrance of roses and romantic candlelit dinners, this account will disappoint.

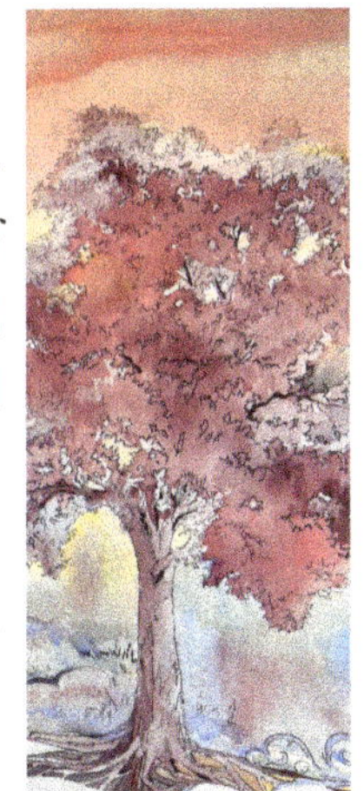

Death is at the heart of this love story. But so is life.

The heartache of a loved one's exit from life is an affront to human sensibility. It can only be calmed by the One with the power to do so.

Jesus.

Raw materials we universally despise—grief, sorrow, and loss have the potential to be transformed by Him into unimaginable joy.

This love story may be disruptive to your senses, but it will still satisfy with a happy ending that is eternal. So go ahead, find that nook for reading, curl up, and sigh in anticipation of an uncommon, true story!

Death will come to all of us. No one from the 1800s is still around. Yet, when loved ones are permanently snatched out of our lives, we are devastated. As humans, we are so contrary! Convincing ourselves that we could not fully live if we dare entertain thoughts of death, we struggle to maintain a perpetual state of youth. Unnamed fears are triggered by the mere possibility of death, so we indulge the pretense that it will never reach us. Faces are slathered with lotions, diets are followed and abandoned, bodies are strengthened in gyms, wrinkles are frowned upon, and frailty of any kind is never admitted to.

And then life is over.

Christians view death differently. We are taught that life on earth is temporal and that eternity awaits. Heaven's joy, without tears or sadness, fills us with hope. And yet, when faced with death, grief is raw and draining. Loss leaves us with an aching void we struggle to fill.

Some never get over it, turning from God in rage or

bitterness. Others mourn, grieve, wander in despair, before returning somewhat diminished. For those once carefree and untroubled, hope becomes a flickering ember likely to be snuffed out by the faintest wind. Faith is dimmed and expectation of God becomes a tattered remnant of what once was.

Not for David nor for Rachel. This is their story.

From Jenny's Funeral

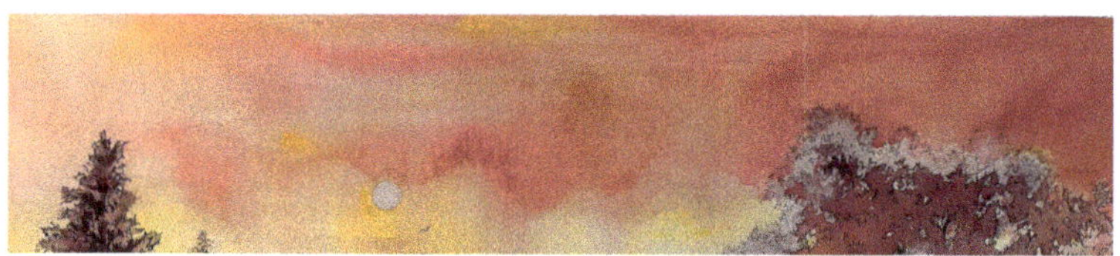

> *"Your worst days are never so bad*
> *that you are beyond*
> *the reach of God's grace*
> *and*
> *Your best days are never so good*
> *that you are beyond*
> *the need of God's grace."*

4

Power Over Death

The Bible fills me with awe. Its words do not merely address the spirit, mind, and body of man, but possess the power to reverse every known human condition, be it sickness, lack, hopelessness, loneliness, fear or, as in this case, grief. The Bible does not merely contain some words *about* God, but every word *is* from God, gifted as a proven remedy for a world of darkness and loss. The mystical concept of Jesus being the Word of God, who became flesh to dwell among us, adds beauty to its power.

I struggle to wrap my mind around it. But I don't really need to. God will help me. He has given me His Spirit so that if I purpose to believe His words, He will do the rest. He will illuminate, instruct, guide, protect and grant me the desire to obey.

He will gift me with special sight to perceive a world unlike any I've known. With Him also rests the power to bless me with days like I've never lived before! And He will do it for anyone who will believe. That is the journey of faith.

David and Rachel walked that walk of faith with Jesus when both of them lost their spouses suddenly, without warning. They did not shake their fist at God and rage or bitterly turn away. They turned to Him. When blinded by tears and trapped in waves of unrelenting grief, He redirected their attention to His goodness.

Impossible, you think? Read on and marvel at God's power to work in human lives when surrendered to Him.

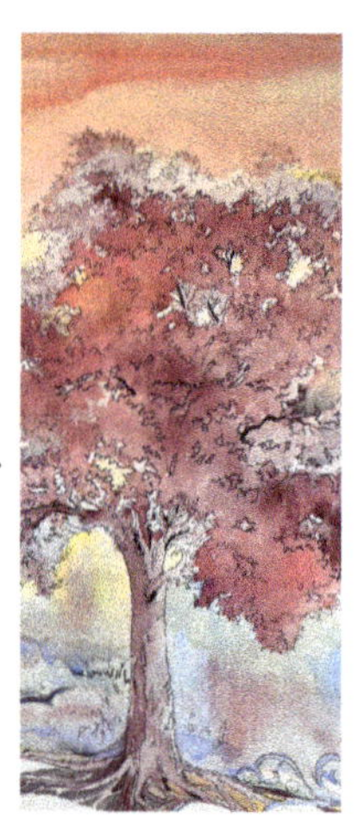

Death has been defanged by Jesus; it it has no power over us, who believe. Some of you may already have experienced the reality of that truth, but for others, perhaps this account will inspire greater faith in the One who calls Himself the Way, the Truth, and the Life.

David has an unusual way with words. Most of this love story is told in words from his journal, which he began a little over a week after Jenny's death. They were married for 25 years.

His writing is peppered with expressions of gratitude

reflected in frequent declarations of how "great-full" to God he was! I did not treat them as typos and correct them, since they expressed his emotion of the moment so well. Only the tangible presence of God with him could have elicited such words of faith. Gratitude is hardly ever witnessed in the throes of grief. Yet it is the fire-escape to rush to, or else sorrow will suffocate with its oppressive power.

I entered their story as an artist, commissioned to create a work of art for his engagement to Rachel. If it were not for her equally steadfast faith, through the loss of her husband, Craig, this love story would never be.

Though my interaction with them was somewhat brief in the timeline of this story, I experienced firsthand their joy through this commission.

The distinctive quality of happiness shared by a bride and bridegroom, especially after a season of captivity by chains of sadness, is described in the Bible as a unique sound expressed in their voices. May my account amplify that melody in visual language, converting sound to sight in praise of God, who made the impossible possible!

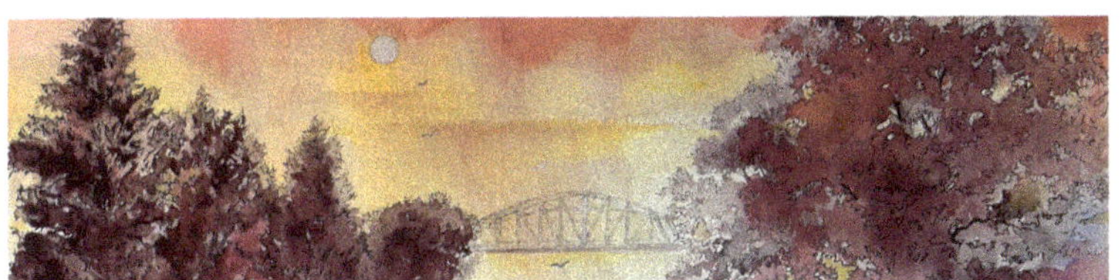

> *'The voice of joy and the voice of gladness,*
> *the voice of the bridegroom and the voice of the bride,*
> *the voice of those who will say:*
> *"Praise the LORD of hosts, for the LORD is good,*
> *For His mercy endures forever"—*
> *and of those who will bring the sacrifice of praise*
> *into the house of the LORD.*
> *For I will cause the captives of the land to return*
> *as at the first,' says the LORD."*
> Jeremiah 33:11 NKJV

David and Rachel are now at the threshold of their future together, but without those with whom they once anticipated sharing their golden years.

They are not destitute—they have Jesus, each other, and a world wide family of faith, known in Christianity as "the body of Christ."

> *"Again, if two lie down together, they will keep warm;*
> *But how can one be warm alone?*
> *Though one may be overpowered by another,*
> *two can withstand him.*
> *And a threefold cord is not quickly broken."*
> Ecclesiastes 4:11-12 NKJV

5

The Art Commission

SARA

One name. Jesus.

He alone is worthy to be praised. So praise I must.

Neither a singer or dancer, I use art materials—paint, clay, charcoal, ink, or an Apple Pencil on an iPad to praise.

Jesus, the Master Artist, creates beauty with everything surrendered to Him. His palette is not limited, and His skill is beyond

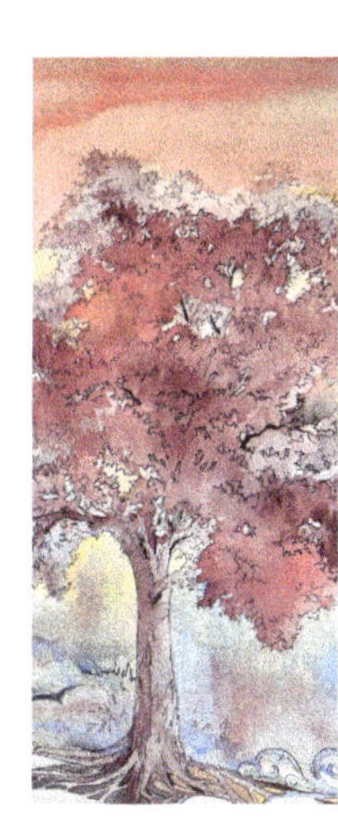

compare. Familiarity with His ways will spark hope for anyone who considers themselves broken beyond redemption.

Working with the best materials known to me I hoped to create an enduring work of art for my clients, David and Rachel. God also worked with them, and for them, with raw materials that are ugly and despised. His results are sweeping, transforming and eternal. Mine will fade and crumble over time. I nurture the hope that my words describing His mastery will endure long enough to help another out of darkness into His light.

"Magnify, glorify and exalt," is His whisper to me, as I struggle to obey with earthly tools and meager ability.

I sense an urgency to offer David's account to alleviate the suffering of others. Time is running out. Despair is sweeping over many in a relentless deluge. Their pain is felt—palpable, festering like an incurable sore. Heavily oppressed people live out their days with furrowed brows and glassy eyes. They need to know that there is hope. Trapped within them is divine capacity for joy and beauty in the midst of a repugnant world. They will remain oblivious in their desperate need unless someone offers them the divine alternative.

David graciously encouraged me to reach them with his story.

Finding myself introspective and sluggish at the start of the year, I was jolted out of my apathy and forced to confront the brevity of life with this commission. Thanksgiving, Christmas, and the New Year festivities passed by in a blur of activity. Suddenly I was propelled into another year before I could even process it. It was supposed to be new, yet it felt like more of the same until this art commission came my way.

I seek the Lord every year in that transition between the old and the new. But this year seemed to follow too closely on the heels of the previous one. I sensed only the familiarity of His sweet presence, not any specific direction as I had hoped. Time either speeds up, or crawls sluggishly, depending on events that intercept our lives. Some seasons of our lives seem to drag on, while moments of delight appear to flash by all too quickly.

It was in this haze that I heard from David, a complete stranger at the time. His email asked if I would be interested in working on an art commission for his upcoming engagement.

Would I ever? Of course! Anything to energize the plodding nature of this new year.

I reminded myself to temper my enthusiasm. I had been disappointed too often and been scammed more than I care to recall. Proceed cautiously, I told myself. I had sadly become a cynic when it came to art commissions.

Creating a process honed over time, I learned to quickly weed out scammers or those who did not respect the rigors of original creative work. I pinned them down to a simple contract. Creative work was only started after the contract was signed and a nonrefundable deposit cleared my bank.

Clients, familiar with my particular creative style, which is easily viewed online, could commission artwork on terms that were more fair to me than they once were. No more wasted hours of fruitless work, nor hopes dashed because of broken promises. Those who did not flinch at my terms became clients.

David promptly agreed and sent me his ideas for a watercolor painting. He moved at a pace faster than I was accustomed to, because he had a swiftly approaching deadline. The artwork was to be a gift for his fiancé, Rachel, when he proposed. And it was soon!

Could I perhaps submit a sketch of the concept that depicted his aspirations for the art? I was to distill my ideas for the painting as a black and white sketch. Keep it simple, I was told, yet with enough finish to be a work of art. After photographing it, he wanted me to send it to him as a high resolution digital image. He then planned to print it out as a quality print and present it to her as a gift. I could send the full color final artwork later.

"Yes, yes, of course," I assured him, without the foggiest idea of what this creative endeavor would entail.

And so began a whirlwind of activity for me, around a single painting that opened the door to another priceless testimony in my journey as an artist, enriched and made meaningful because of Jesus.

Paintings already convey stories. Somehow, this time the art felt insufficient. Although my clients were delighted with the finished artwork, I sensed that the richness of this account could not be left unexpressed. What a shame to not share this couple's triumph with the world!

Words were needed to paint the sadness, joy, faith and hope, all connected by the golden arc of the presence of Jesus. This, their story, is narrated from my perspective, but using their words and those of many others, who form the flesh and blood cast of this love story.

Unlike the filtered polish of social media posts, the words in this account are authentic. They capture the unguarded moments that express the depths of the human heart as it grapples with life in all its complexity. As you read, remind yourself that this is a true account with only the names changed to respect their privacy.

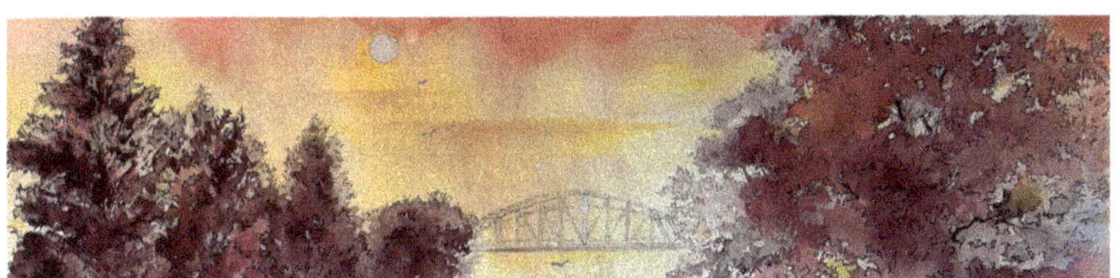

6

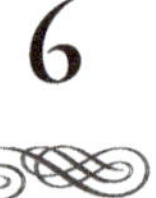

David

David is an artist at heart.

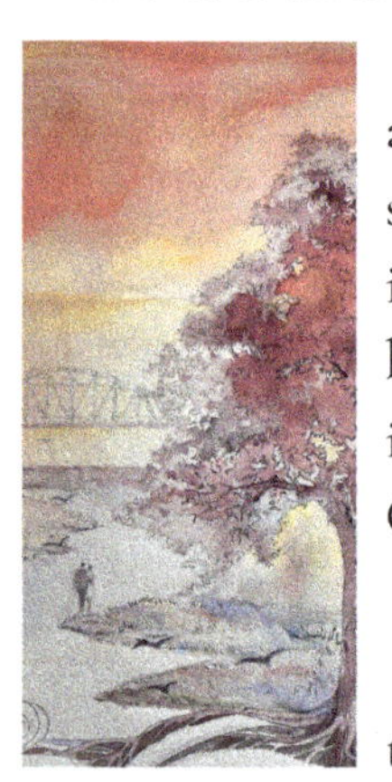

He told me that he "tried art school" and abandoned it in frustration. He felt that his skill was inadequate to express the complexity of his ideas. Deciding that execution was best left to others—"real artists," as he put it, he pursued a more sensible career as the CEO of a technology company.

His artistic temperament and exposure to the mechanics of art creation made him an ideal client. I was delighted that this was someone who understood my challenges and would truly appreciate the effort I put into the artwork.

The poetry of words and the richness of music moves him.

"Shadows of the Dawn" by *Gray Havens* was a song that articulated what he wanted embodied in the final artwork.

Unfamiliar with it, I hurriedly looked it up online. Reading the lyrics as the music washed over me, filled me with the certainty that the love that David and Rachel shared was a holy work of God. It humbled me to play this small role in their moving story of redemption.

David's dynamic, gregarious nature extracted from me more than I dreamed I could deliver, in a far shorter time than I usually set aside for art commissions. There was a deadline and it was a joyous one. How could I not hurry?

In telling their story, I have maintained, as much as possible, the integrity of their words, gleaned from journals, memorial services and other materials. This is a faithful account of their emotions of pain, grief and joy. However, for ease of reading, I did edit their words a little as I saw fit.

David's words, and those of colleagues, family and friends, describe one aspect of the work of God. My art yet another. The music and the lyrics that he sent me added another dimension to the account. The copyright of the musicians prevent me from including the lyrics here; but they can easily be accessed online.

However, nothing can match the "WORK" that God wrought in both him and Rachel. Attempting to describe the creativity of that masterful endeavor is an exercise in futility. It is better to let you decide for yourself.

Solomon in Ecclesiastes said it best.

> *"Then I saw all the work of God,*
> *that a man cannot find out the work*
> *that is done under the sun.*
> *For though a man labors to discover it,*
> *yet he will not find it;*
> *moreover, though a wise man*
> *attempts to know it,*
> *he will not be able to find it."*
> Ecclesiastes 8:17 NKJV

7

Denial

DAVID: THURSDAY, JULY 7, 2022

8 Days After Jenny's Death

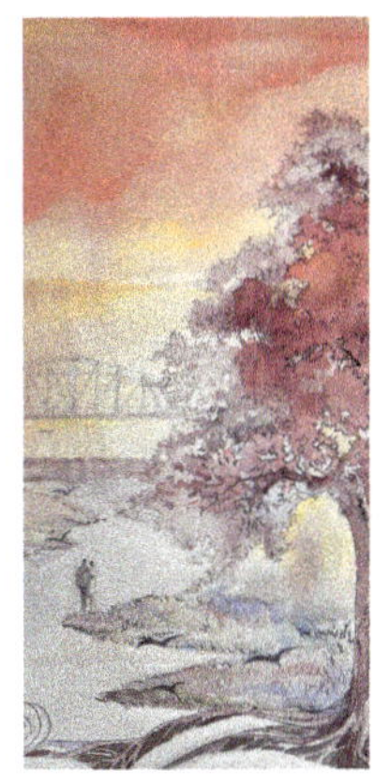

So where am I this morning?

In DENIAL.

I don't know that I still have wrapped my mind around the fact that Jenny is not here. The suddenness! I think I am in shock. I start each morning crying out to God for His peace and comfort. It hurts so bad!

I regret that I didn't appreciate the gift that God gave me in her the way I should have. I tried. But I could have, and should have, done so much more. I know that it's not healthy to linger in this mindset. I am just being honest about where I am right now.

FRIDAY, JULY 8, 2022

On Wednesday night, sitting without Jenny at church immediately brought to mind thoughts of the numerous occasions I prioritized my work over the service and left her seated alone. It hurts to know how lonely she must have felt. It fills me with regret!

I start each morning reading through her devotional and her Bible study notes. What precious memories she left behind to encourage me, as she explored the treasure she had in Christ!

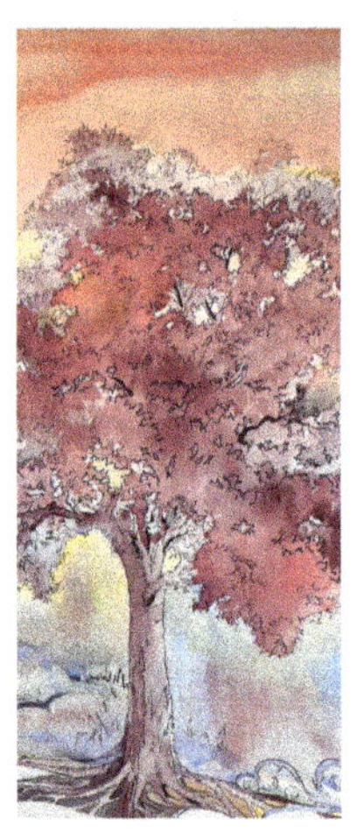

I then take time to look through her photos. I scan each picture intently to see her eyes and her million watt smile. I listen to the videos to hear her voice. Oh, how my heart aches, and the tears flow, as my mind is flooded with memories!

I am so thankful to God that He entrusted her to me. I just wish I had her a bit longer.

My heart cries out. I can't do this. I need the help, grace and comfort that He has promised.

I am still in shock, working through my regrets and overwhelmed by the outpouring of love being shown to our family. At the same time, I do feel the peace and comfort from God. I continue to find that His grace IS sufficient.

SUNDAY, JULY 10, 2022

In reviewing Jenny's Bible study notes for what feels like the umpteenth time, I can't get her last entry out of my mind. She was studying the book of Colossians. Her final entry starts with the verse below.

> *"For Christ is the end of the law for righteousness to every one that believes."*
> Romans 10:4 NKJV

She penned a reminder to herself that she must put off the dead body of her sinful flesh.

Then she wrote,
"Dead ——— Forgiveness ——— Alive with Christ!"

The tears flow as I just sit looking at this page!

I know with certainty that she is now alive with Christ! She wouldn't want to come back, but the sting of death is real and it hurts!

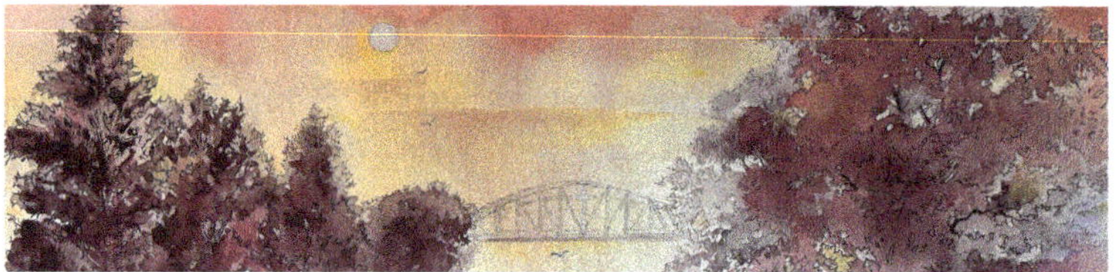

8

Last Date With Jenny

DAVID

THURSDAY, JULY 20, 2022

Jenny's birthday is Friday.

My heart is heavy and my eyes fill as I think of all the wonderful birthdays God gave us in the past 25 years.

I recall our last date night. It was the night before her death.

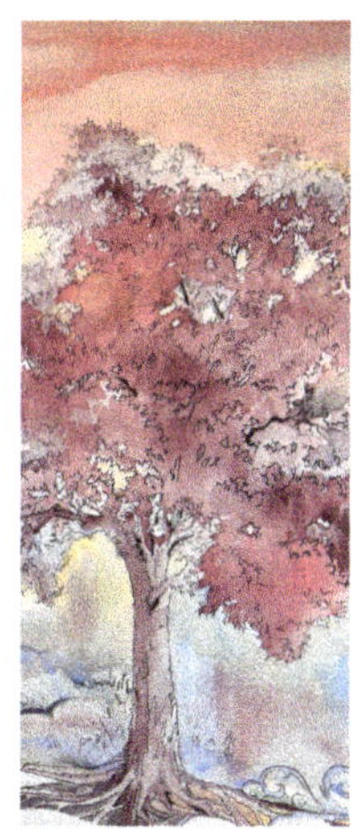

She was recovering from back surgery. We drove slowly to Chick-fil-A for an ice cream cone. I held her hand as we drove.

She reminded me to drive carefully over the bumps as we returned to the house.

I know we serve a sovereign God. We are in His hands and only He can provide comfort. As I lie here reflecting on these past few weeks, I stand in awe of God's goodness to me and my family! He has provided strength for each day. He has increased my desire to know Him more and sent people to encourage and pray for me!

This morning's devotional focused on our inheritance in Christ.

> *"Blessed be the God and Father of our Lord Jesus Christ,*
> *which according to his abundant mercy*
> *hath begotten us again unto a lively hope*
> *by the resurrection of Jesus Christ from the dead,*
> *To an inheritance incorruptible, and undefiled,*
> *and that fadeth not away, reserved in heaven for you... "*
> 1 Pet. 1:3-4. KJV

As I reflect on that, I am so great-full for His love for me! I am undeserving, yet He extends love, mercy and a priceless inheritance. Nothing in the world that I build, or do, will last. Only the eternal work of Christ will endure.

Oh, how that challenges me to step over the little things

that don't matter to point everyone to Christ, so that they also might have an eternal inheritance—a real relationship with Christ.

Without His constant care for me these past weeks, I would be in a hospital! Yet this morning, I was out of my hotel room by 5:45 a.m. and made my way to McDonald's for coffee. I started my day with *Sovereign Grace* music to feed my soul. A friend texted me *"Though You Slay Me"* by *Shane and Shane*—a perfect song that mirrors Job's trial that I had studied yesterday!

The day was very busy, but wrapped up early enough for me to make the drive home at a reasonable hour. When I arrived home, I was greeted warmly, or rather, was run over by my puppies, who smothered me with puppy kisses.

A pile of cards awaited me inside. What love was expressed as many remarked about Jenny's birthday—how she had touched their lives and how grateful to God they were for her!

She so loved God and was always striving to become more like Him. Best of all, she brought people with her on her journey! She was a true gift!

May I be a follower of Christ is this same manner. May God give me boldness to share my faith. May I see those around me, who are hurting, and be a listening ear and a helping hand. May I have opportunity to tell them about my great God, who has given me such peace, comfort and JOY in the midst of my grief!

FRIDAY, JULY 21, 2022

Jenny's 1st birthday in heaven! Happy birthday, Love!

Thursday night's sleep came in the form of a small nap at 3 a.m. and then I was wide wake at 4:30. I lay in bed reflecting on so many treasured memories, listening to *Sovereign Grace* music!

> *"Blessed be the God and Father of our Lord Jesus Christ"*
> (1 Pet. 1:3) KJV

The written words of God encourage and sustain me. I have an amazing church, filled with fellow believers that God uses to comfort me and my family! How can I not bless His name and shout His praise? He is doing a work in my heart and giving me eyes to see the needs of others. He gives me grace and strength every time I ask!

Lord, I can't do this!

I so desperately need you and your strength. I don't know

what today will bring me, but I know you do, so please let my heart rest in you, knowing that you will provide the strength I need to navigate the day ahead!

The girls and I took a detour to Chick-fil-A for breakfast and were in the office by 7:15 a.m.

I bring Jenny's devotional diary with me to work and keep it close by. As I navigate the day, if I find my mind going in the wrong direction by becoming filled with self pity, I open the diary and remind myself of the truth of God's word.

It comforts me and guides my mind back to dwelling on His limitless grace and strength!

The first wave hit me at 8:30 a.m. Cole came into my office and sensed that my mind was keenly tuned to this being Jenny's birthday. I now see Cole, and his dear wife, as if we are back at the funeral home and the tears just flow! He sat with me for a good hour to encourage me.

Once home, I sat down and wrote this list of God's grace to me as I reflected on my Jenny's death.

How gracious God was that He

- gave me a wife, who loved God deeply and drew others in that they might also love Him more
- gave us a Pastor, who so lovingly points us to the truth

and reminds us of the deep relationship we can have in Christ

- gave Jenny Zoe, an accountability partner and a true friend
- placed Jenny's church office next to Pastor's so that they might share many hours of conversation
- gave us our daughters. Jenny tirelessly pointed them to Christ and planted in them the desire to love and serve our great God
- gave Jenny her sister, who was so close—a very special relationship
- gave Jenny a cancer scare—this event grew her faith and increased her dependence on God.

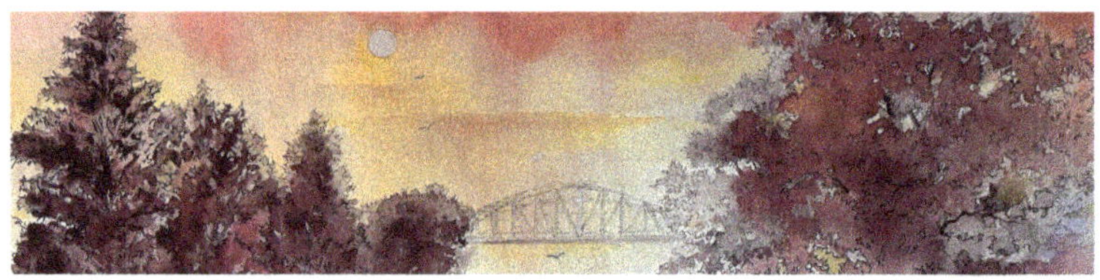

9

The Cancer Scare

DAVID'S JOURNAL, CHRISTMAS 2021

"I went into planning for this Christmas as if it was my last Christmas. I didn't know if I had cancer or not, so I planned for this one as if it was my last one," Jenny told me.

After Christmas, we rejoiced in God's goodness when we found out it was not cancer!

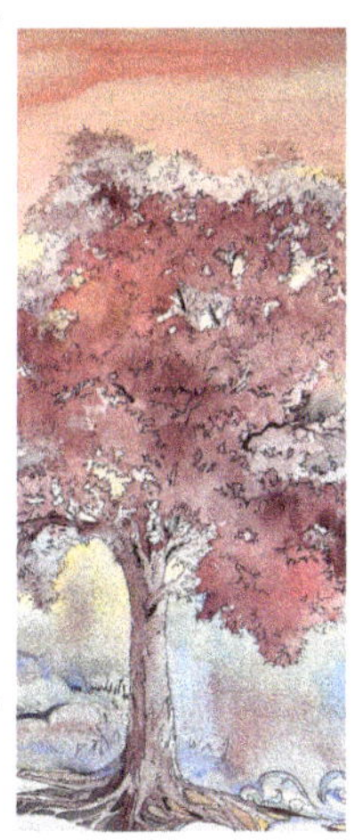

That was when the second wave of grief hit me! We were rejoicing that it was not our last Christmas, but it actually was.

Jenny prepared like she never had before.

Now Luke and Clara look out their back door and say, *"Wow, how good is God to stir Mom's heart to bless me in this way!"*

Liz and Noah look in their bedroom downstairs and reflect on God's goodness—all the little extra things that she blessed us with. Her gifts were so very thoughtful and now even more special to us all! How gracious is our God to give us such a beautiful memory of a very special Christmas!

Liz and Noah had a terrific wedding—great memories, captured so well by the wedding photographer! We were all together, which was one of Jenny's wishes and what she most enjoyed.

What a privilege it was to be her helper through her recovery—that closeness, as I attended to her hour by hour needs!

During her recovery, once out of bed, I cherish the memory of the daily walks on the driveway, the walks to the pool to get sun on her legs—to feel human again. Then, there was our last dinner, on the night before her death. We ate next to the pool.

What a special time our ice cream date night in the car was— that very night before her death!

On the morning of her death, after she got out of the

shower, I rubbed lotion on her feet and on her legs. I had to quickly cover her feet as Hazel's (the puppy) tongue was hastily removing the lotion!

Finally, there was the afternoon call, just 30 minutes before she died.

"I love you," I said.

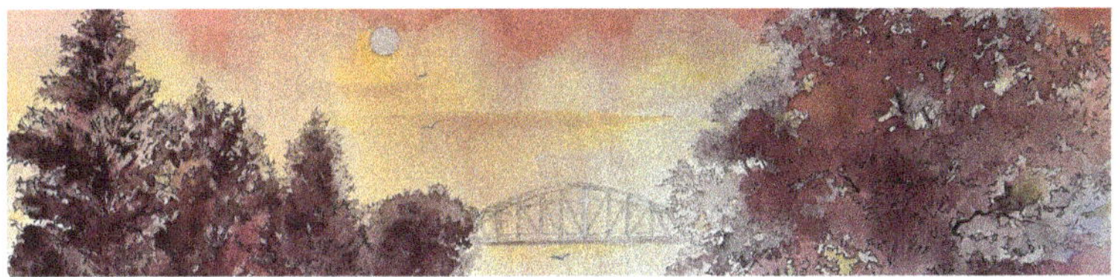

IO

I Know Her!

SARA

I've never met Jenny. And yet the strange sense of *"I know her,"* that inexplicable leap of recognition, catches me off guard as I watch a video created by her family as a loving tribute. I don't doubt that I will one day meet her as eternity also welcomes me. In the meantime, there is still that certain sense of connectedness.

The uniting presence of the indwelling Holy Spirit is the only explanation for this unusual sensation of knowing a stranger—a bond that transcends time and space.

Haven't you experienced it before? Someone, who loves Jesus, feels closer, even if your encounter with them was brief, than those you've known your whole life, who do not yet know Him. There is a spirit to spirit recognition. We are people of similar faith that the Bible declares is precious in the sight of God.

Jenny's smile is mirrored on the happy faces of her twin daughters. I am drawn by her easy grace and energy. She is now part of the *"great cloud of witnesses."* I will one day join them.

In her memorial video, she fills the screen with her vitality. I watch her playing with her puppies, taking selfies, giggling with her daughters and leaning back against her beloved husband, David. She loved and is loved.

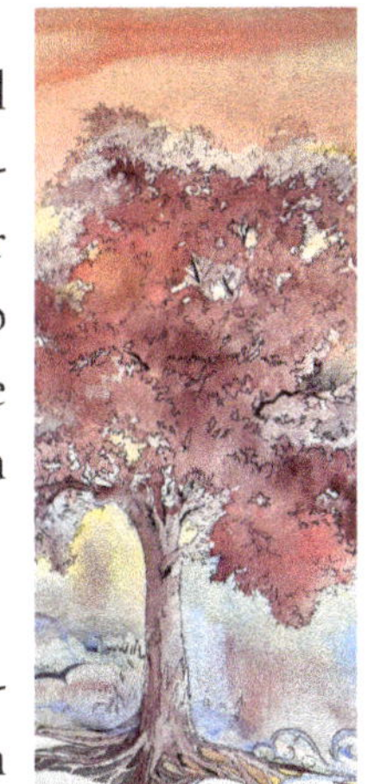

I intuitively sense that she was exceptional in all the roles she played, whether daughter, wife, mother, coach, business woman or mentor. That was an easy conclusion; not so obvious was that her excellence was because she energetically strode through life in an authentic relationship with Jesus.

She surely had her faults, but the gentleness of her spirit fairly leaped off the screen without a hint of any marring flaw.

David told me that on June 29, 2022, Jenny stepped outside to collect her mail and never made it back to her earthly home. She died from complications of a back surgery from which she fully expected to recover. She had hoped to cuddle her yet to be born grandchild. However, that was not to be.

In a moment of time, unexpected and harsh in its arrival for those left behind, she stepped into the heaven that she had only read about in her Bible. She saw the face of Jesus, who she had loved and served wholeheartedly all her earthly life. For her it was the ultimate victory. For those who loved her it was a loss they had to triumph over with Jesus.

She was only in her forties.

Jenny was David's bride for 25 years, the mother of his twins, Liz and Clara, who were married to Noah and Luke respectively.

Laura was the much awaited, as yet unborn, grandchild.

I I

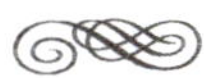

Jesus in My Process

SARA

I am not unfamiliar with adventures in art with Jesus. We are a team. I respond to His prompting and listen earnestly for His voice during the process of art making. If you were to picture our partnership, it would look a bit like this.

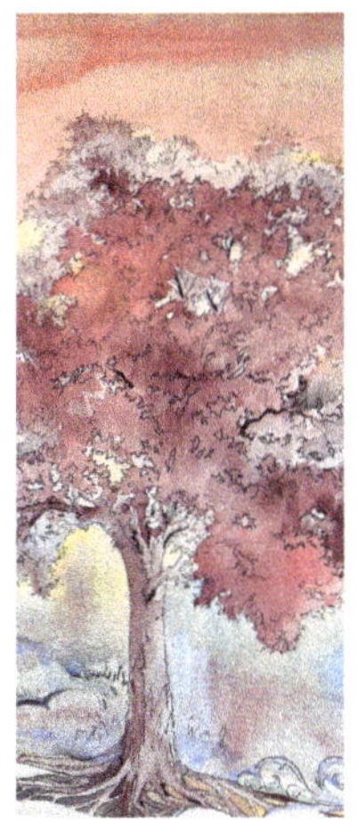

Clenched in the fist of a little girl is a crayon. She has never grown up, nor does she ever want to, preferring to retain her wonder and curiosity of the world around her. Yet she wants to be an artist and create beauty. There's just one problem, she doesn't have the faintest clue how to go about it.

He does.

He fills her spirit with His light, wraps His hand around her fingers and helps her draw. She loves the process, leaning against His shoulder and watching in awe as He creates shapes she never could. She is continually fascinated by what appears from her hands.

He speaks to her in ways she can understand and guides her in the many choices that result in works of art—choices of colors, texture, line and shape. He wisely coaxes her to relax the tightness of her grip and she yields to His skill. He is the Master Artist.

He lets her pretend she is the artist that she has always wanted to be. She knows better and loves Him for indulging her!

She is convinced that He leaves the best for last. After she has gone to bed, He fixes bad passages of paintings where she insisted on her own way, taking care to leave behind enough of an imprint of her efforts so that her work still carries the sense of it being her own. The completed artwork always reflects so much more than her own ability and she knows that. That is how kind He is!

He stoops to help and I am helped. That is how we work, Jesus and I. If that were all, I would be so grateful.

But there's more—more, for which I have few words that can articulate my awe.

He somehow permits the finished art to speak to others in His language. As they view the work, He grants them hope, brings to mind His promises and reminds them of His faithfulness. As long as the artwork exists and someone pauses to view it, He will speak.

These are thoughts too grand for the little girl who put her hand to the work—thoughts that never crossed her mind.

To be granted this partnership is a source of joy to me. I am continually filled with wonder at what He tells others (and me!) through the language of beauty and art. Art is visual speech, which when yielded to Jesus, will touch the depths of the human spirit.

To take any credit would be ludicrous! How could I? I am just an artist in service to the Master Artist.

His ability takes that which is beautiful and enhances it further. All artists strive to do that in some measure, but He does more, on levels beyond our comprehension. The ugly, raw, painful, terrifying, and hopeless moments of life are also viable raw materials in His hands. He possesses the wondrous skill of transforming those qualities that artists would shun into complete works of exquisite beauty.

And His finished product is a joy to behold in multiple

dimensions—like viewing a diamond in different settings with different lighting—soft or harsh, diffused or focussed. It flashes with unmatched brilliance from every angle—an expression of breathtaking perfection, the indubitable work of a Master Artist.

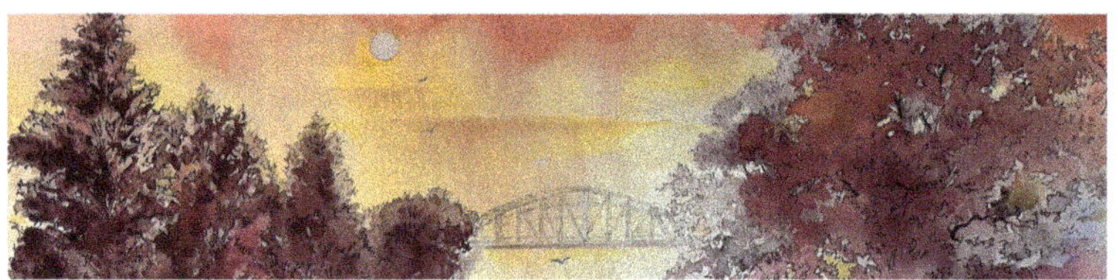

12

Psalm 34

I started my morning reviewing my photos of Jenny. I so LOVE her freckles—that picture from the lake, where it's 97 inside the house! Her sweet face shows the beauty of God's handiwork.

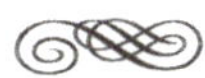

What a gift she was—and to so many people, not just me! She made me feel like it was just me. I know how she tolerated my impulsiveness—it was through God's grace. I long wondered how, and why. Now I rejoice for the grace that sustained her as she often confronted and slowed me down. She knew that it would require so much energy and time to do so, yet she kept at it!

Today I have a challenge. Kent challenged us to memorize Psalm 34, a beautiful passage and a comforting reminder during this time. I think I heard Iris, Doug, and Pastor refer to it at the funeral.

I wrote out the first 12 verses in Jenny's devotional journal that I take with me everywhere. I left the page open all day. As thoughts creep in seeking to wreck me, I remind myself of God's truth.

> *1 "I will bless the Lord at all times;*
> *His praise shall continually be in my mouth.*
> *2 My soul will make its boast in the Lord;*
> *The humble will hear it and rejoice.*
> *3 Exalt the Lord with me,*
> *And let's exalt His name together."*
> Psalm 34:1-3 NKJV

Reflecting on this throughout the day gave me such courage, grace and strength!

Liz and Clara were back in the office today and I took great joy in placing a big kiss on their foreheads each time I passed their desks, throughout the day.

On the drive home I worked on memorizing verses 1-3 of Psalm 34.

Tomorrow I start my road trip to Michigan with a good friend and client. I'll get
back on Friday afternoon. I needed to find
someone to watch my girls (his dogs) and
was so excited that a dear lady in our church,
who is also a dog lover, was willing to stay
in our home with them. I was able to walk
her through their routine and am looking
forward to them making a new friend with
her golden lab!

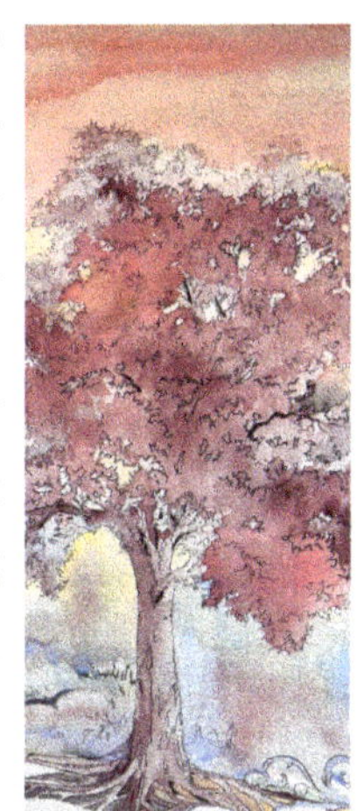

In the evening, I spent some time on a
call with our dear friend, Dr. Campbell. He is the back sur-
geon who did Jenny's surgery. On the drive home, I couldn't
get him out of my mind as I worked through the verses in
Psalm 34.

I spent time assuring him that I loved him and do not
hold anything against him. As a doctor, I knew he would be
playing more "What if..." games than I was. And he was!

I encouraged him to think rightly about Jenny's home
going—that her purpose here on earth was complete. While
we don't fully know that purpose, we rest in God's grace,
knowing that *no good thing will He withhold from them that
walk uprightly"* Psalm 84:11 KJV

I then shared how God was already using Jenny's home
going to point so many members of our church into deeper

relationships in their homes, encouraging them to take up their walk with Christ with more urgency and purpose.

We finished the night with Kent and Iris coming over and playing Jenny's favorite card game as we reflected on God's grace!

I pray that I will be patient, and that God will continue to draw me to Himself so that I may walk closer.

WEDNESDAY, JULY 13, 2022

I started my day reviewing the photo album of Jenny. This time I watch the videos as well so I can hear her voice. My eyes immediately fill with tears. Oh, how I miss my Love!

As I reflect through my day yesterday, I am reminded of just how well she cared for me and others. She thought through every nuance of a decision—swiftly, yet fully considering how that decision would impact others. She also prevented many actions of mine. I would call to ask about doing something and she would quickly tell me the reasons why not, or why not now.

Yesterday I was also confronted with the fact that there will be many firsts for us all in the days ahead!

My morning included a nice, tension relieving visit to my

massage therapist. Then the day was full at work, where I got lots of hugs from Liz and Clara and plenty of puppy kisses from Hazel!

I was able to take a small nap in between meetings to help me be prepared for the late drive to Grand Rapids, Michigan. The theme through the day was a combination of reflecting on Psalm 34, reminding myself of my GREAT GOD, and remembering how well my Jenny loved and supported me.

Her drive and work ethic both in, and outside the home, was a thing of beauty! Every step was filled with purpose as she maximized her time. Then, after a full day, she would finally sit down at around 10 p.m. with her cup of coffee and watch her home shows!

I so miss her, and this week as I travel, I will miss checking in on her and hearing her voice of encouragement. I will miss her excitement as she shares her pictures and tells me of an amazing deal she found, or shares how God is moving in a young girl's life as she works through a book study with her.

I pray for grace and that God will continue to draw me to Himself to refine me be who He wants me to be.

THURSDAY, JULY 14, 2022

God gave me 8 hours of sleep last night!

Today I again start my day reviewing my picture album. I find myself zooming in on her lovely face. I study the emotions reflected there. With each video my heart aches so badly every time I hear her dear voice.

As I reached the end of my time, a school Principal from a very small school in Tennessee called. It was a school to which Jenny had taken her volleyball team at the beginning of each season for a tournament. He was calling to check in on me. My voice was telling him I was a wreck!

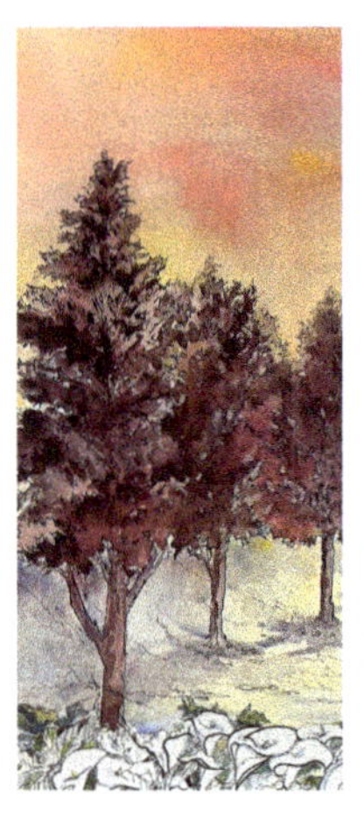

I went on to tell him of my daily process of purposefully grieving and reflecting on my Jenny. He was catching me at the end of my daily time.

As I regained composure, I shared with him how my heart aches, yet how God was giving me the strength to stand. There is no way I can do this on my own!

Recalling that he has adopted children of his own, I went on to encourage him to do the hard work of loving his children, showing them God's goodness and grace.

I told him to stop thinking about what people around him thought of him and to serve his family well. I pleaded with him to remember that his children need to see Christ through him in the way that he serves them.

13

❦❧

The Pursuit of Beauty

SARA

I delight in working with multiple media, from clay to graphite, in my pursuit of beauty as an artist. I am acutely aware that quality materials produce quality work.

As artists, we have been taught to invest in the best we can afford. We dare not sabotage our efforts by resorting to cheap supplies. Mere skill cannot bridge the divide between juicy, brilliant colors and pasty, chalky hues of cheap paints. Watercolors must be the finest to produce transparent washes of glowing color, or else the result will be a disappointingly dull painting.

Thin, absorbent paper is inexpensive, but will buckle at the first drop of water. On the other hand, heavy, sized paper holds color in a luminescent embrace on a surface that will remain as tight as a drum, regardless of how much water is floated over it. The weight of the paper matters. Of course, the heavier the paper, the costlier it becomes. Quality paper has the added bonus of not yellowing over time, as it is free of acids that will consume it from within.

Which artist does not dream that their art will endure long past their lifetime in cherished collections of avid collectors? Artists are dreamers, and I sometimes suspect that I am the most fanciful! I don't dream for myself, but to be a witness for Jesus, who deserves my best—the longest, most enduring, artistic declaration I can make, testifying somehow to His goodness until it can speak no longer!

When my art goes the way of all the world, from ashes to ashes, dust to dust, becoming dull as the paper crumbles, I would like to hope that it left with a shout of praise in the air and not with a whimper!

I am an ordinary artist, one of countless in the world. I often fight the many voices in my head that argue about the exorbitant cost of art materials and the corresponding urgency to create worthy artwork. By His grace and lavish supply, I somehow procure the best materials possible and diligently apply myself to the craft.

I leave the aspect of worth up to Him to whom I entrust

all my efforts. I can do no less nor more. In this fallen world I am helpless, except for the One who is faithful to help whenever I turn to Him—which is often!

In contrast to my meager efforts at art, the Master Artist, Jesus, spares no expense and creates works of indescribable beauty. He gave His life, who can give more?

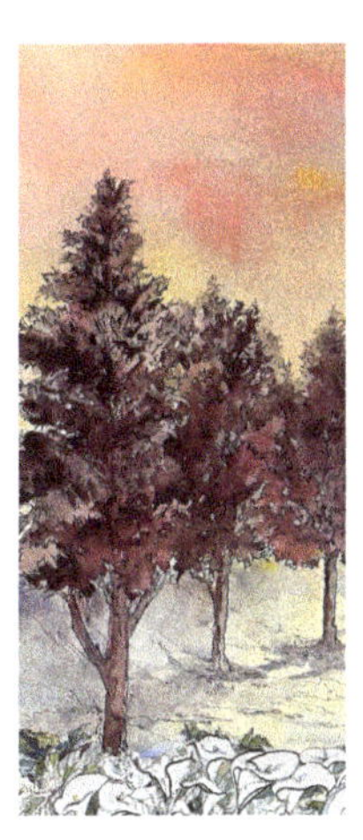

That He creates incredible beauty in nature is evident everywhere I turn. I became an artist because I knew that the beauty of nature would engross me. It would happily keep me as a lifetime captive in art, without ever waning in fervor or passion. I am not writing about that kind of beauty in this account.

This time I was taken aback by the different kind of beauty reflected in David and Rachel's stories. Heartbreaking loss will one day smother all happy lives, often without even the whisper of a warning. We live in a fallen world and cannot escape death.

When the lives of David and Rachel were devastated by the sudden deaths of their beloved spouses, it would have been reasonable to wonder what possible good could come from the utter darkness that visited them.

Nothing, if it were not for the work of the Master Artist!

What He wrought is beautiful, and impossible to duplicate by any human means.

I showed up, with my earthly took kit of materials, on assignment to create a single visual statement to commemorate His exquisite skill! My work is destined to fade away. His will last for eternity. That's how insignificant my role was in this. I am the tiny dot—the "period," at the end of His praiseworthy poem!

I marvel at the blessing of being permitted to peer through the windows of two different households as they grappled with their loss.

Art drew me closer into the lives, and loves, of two strangers to see the Master Artist's process of walking them through to victory. It blessed me immensely and I pray it will you also.

That is beauty that no human can capture, let alone create!

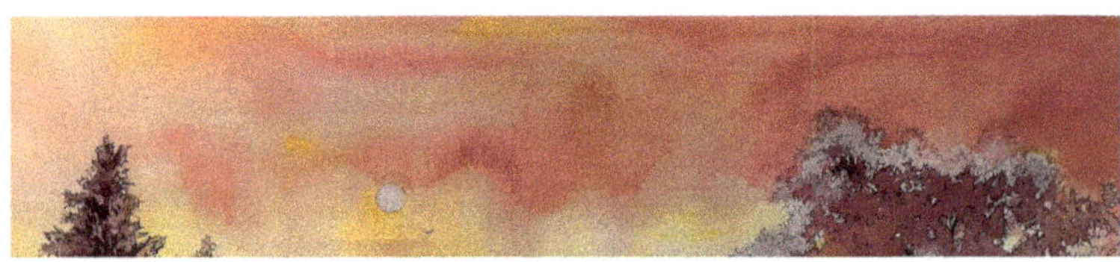

I4

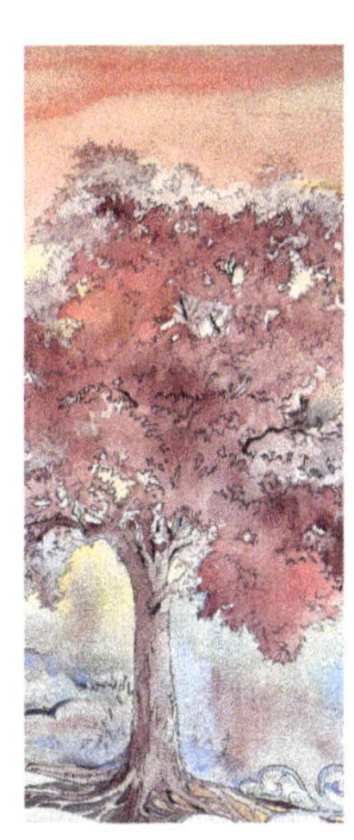

Rachel

On March 13, 2020, three years before David lost Jenny, Rachel's husband, Craig, unexpectedly reached the end of his journey here on earth and stepped into the arms of his Savior, Jesus. An aortic dissection caused him his final heart beat on earth.

He was only forty four.

Rachel was now solely responsible for the care of their teenage son, Levi, and daughter, Emma. She had become a widow suddenly and without warning.

Three years later, listening to her share her excitement with me, about the painting commissioned by David, I sensed a woman of strength, whose life had been transformed because of a close walk with Jesus through circumstances none of us would ever wish for. Her soft voice masked a core of steel that I knew she possessed.

Tried by the fires of her ordeal, she had emerged as pure gold. I remember reading somewhere that a refiner's cue for extracting metal at peak purity from the fire was when he could see his clear reflection on its shimmering surface. I do not doubt that Jesus saw Himself in her, since I could as well.

In our conversation I sensed the profound humility of a life surrendered to Him. His comforting presence had brought her to this joyous season of her life, planning a wedding with David—an occasion that she could never have envisioned during the dark seasons of her grief. She bore little resemblance to the teary, but composed, woman I watched in the recording of Craig's home going service, three years earlier.

Covid restrictions prevented Craig's memorial service from being held right after his death. Five months of grieving later, the family was finally permitted to gather together, socially distanced in their church sanctuary. They shared their remembrances, dedicated thanksgiving, and worshipped God for his life.

Craig had often declared that he was "*a worshipper consumed with knowing God intimately and actively cultivating spiritual growth.*" The photos of him filling the large screen in the sanctuary exuded the quiet confidence of one who pursued God and found delight in his pursuit. His decision to follow Jesus was made at thirteen, when most teenagers are consumed with just about everything else. Judging from the words that others now spoke about him, spiritual maturity was evident in his life, three decades of cultivation later.

As slides moved smoothly from one image to another, I saw a doting father, a passionate husband, a patient teacher, an outdoorsman, a skilled musician and so much more. A man's life cannot be told in slides, although they do offer a snapshot of who he was.

He had a passion for sweet desserts served in insanely large portions! Ice cream scoops piled high against the backdrop of his happy face filled the screen, a silent visual of the simple pleasures of life.

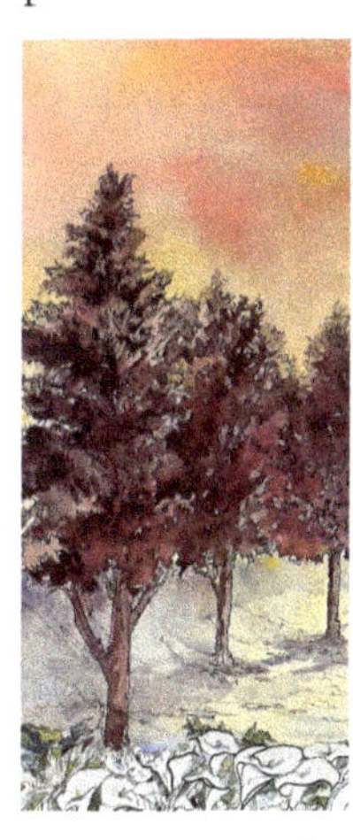

Music was his language of praise and the trombone was his instrument of choice. He earned his Master's degree from the University of Nebraska, Lincoln, and also had a Doctorate of Musical Arts degree from the University of Minnesota. In his brief life, he breathed music, played in chamber music orchestras, freelanced as a musician, and served as his church Orchestra Director. In 2003, he became the Chair of the Music Department of a private Christian university, in St. Paul.

He had even more accomplishments that were lauded by

many in the service. To me, he was exceptional not due to human accolades, but because it was apparent that he served God with passion and integrity.

The verse below captures the enigma of a quality that is indefinable—the mark of Jesus on a human life. David, Jenny, Rachel and Craig all carried that trait. So did Peter and John, Jesus' disciples, who lived out their brief lives over two thousand years ago. Even though their lives were vastly different, separated in time, culturally and geographically, they were marked by the intimacy of time spent with Jesus.

> *"Now when they saw the boldness of Peter and John, and perceived that they were unlearned and ignorant men, they marveled; and they took knowledge of them, that they had been with Jesus."* Act 4:13 NKJV

Academic credentials are not inconsequential; they are to be celebrated! However, there is something about being with Jesus, which confers boldness, a subtle confidence and uncommon calmness, no matter the circumstance. Many tributes by family and colleagues spoke of Craig possessing such qualities in spades. I imagine that Rachel found him to be the rock that she could always depend on, until they were quietly parted in death.

Dressed in a simple black dress of mourning, Rachel

spoke in a voice that had the catch of tears in it. Her teenage children, wearing masks, listened from their places on the front row, seated separate from the others. Their lives would never be the same again. On such a traumatic day, to stand up before family and friends to offer her thanksgiving to God for Craig's life took great courage.

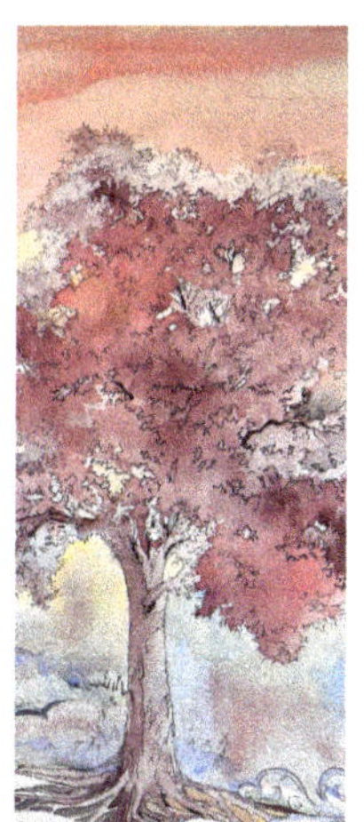

"On Friday, March 13, when I realized that something was seriously wrong, I cried out to God with Psalm 46, verses one and two," she began.

"I am thankful how God brought those words to my mind at that moment. He reminded me that He was our refuge," her voice broke, *"and strength, a very present help in trouble. We will not fear."*

She paused and then read out the first five verses of Psalm 46.

I listened.

Her voice grew stronger as she read.

By the time she reached the last word I heard her steely resolve to depend on Him, which would keep her through her trial, until the mourning was past and God's gift of joy was once more hers to enjoy.

> [[To the chief Musician for the sons of Korah,
> A Song upon Alamoth.]]
> *"God is our refuge and strength,
> a very present help in trouble."*
> Psalm 46:1KJV

I love looking up the meanings and use of Hebrew words to better understand context and intent of the Psalmist. So I did a quick search for the meaning of the word "Alamoth" in the Blue Letter Bible and it seems to refer to the voice of a woman, a soprano! How appropriate.

> *"Therefore will not we fear, though the earth be removed,
> and though the mountains be carried
> into the midst of the sea;
> Though the waters thereof roar and be troubled,
> though the mountains shake with the swelling thereof.
> Selah.
> There is a river, the streams whereof shall make glad
> the city of God, the holy place of the tabernacles of
> the most High. God is in the midst of her;
> she shall not be moved: God shall help her... "*
> Psalm 46:2-5 KJV

Without a doubt, she saw herself as a city in trouble, besieged by the roar of mountains crashing into the sea, while the ground on which she stood was shaking. It brought terror to her soul!

Yet she would choose to not fear. She would choose to trust in the river of God's grace to propel her to His dwelling place, where she would eventually find joy. Her spirit invited Him into the midst of her nightmare, to secure her footing and bring her through, even as her voice quietly read and cherished the words.

And He did.

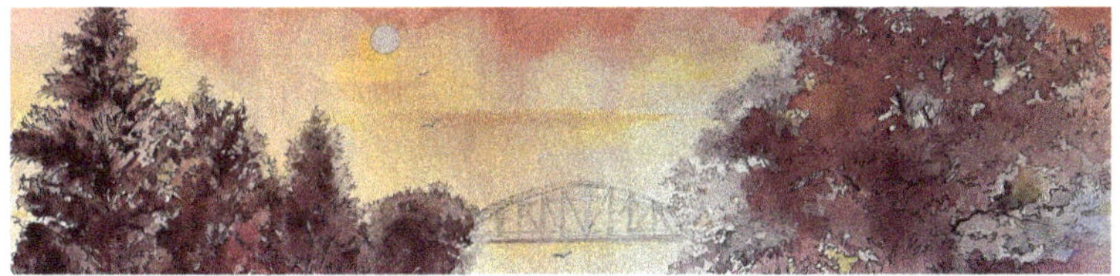

15

❦

The Platform of the Trial

DAVID: JULY 14, 2022

I am in Grand Rapids, Michigan, today doing a site visit at a long term care nursing home that also has assisted living. My client will be purchasing this facility and I am here to learn how the technology is configured and what technology is needed prior to the purchase date.

The IT (Information Technology) team from the seller's side is a group of four guys. I spent three hours with one of them as he walked me through the facility. He was a sharp, young man and we built a rapport fairly quickly. Once I was done, I sat down in an open area, just a few tables from his IT team to begin my documentation process.

As I sat, I began to catch up on emails and texts. I then came across a text from Anna that caught my eye. She sent over a quote from a book she was reading

"Rather than resist the hardships that God brings into your life, embrace them as good gifts from His hand, meant to deepen you and to expand your influence for His glory. Instead of letting today's hardship come down on top of you, climb on top of it, and shout God's goodness from the platform of your trial."

I swallowed hard after reading this and my eyes filled with tears! I can't do this, only God can.

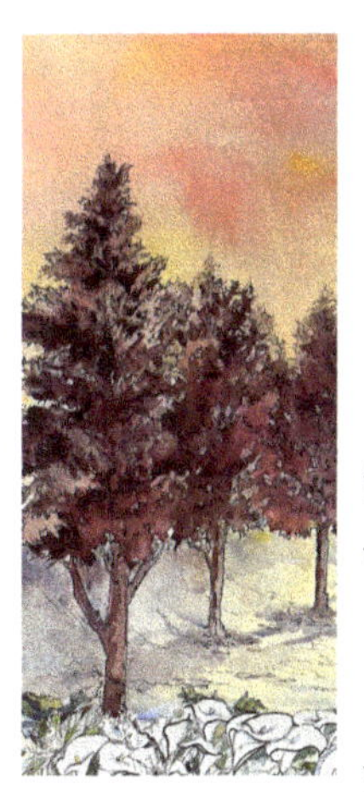

But will He?

Will I?

I was torn as I reflected on this quote for a minute, and then I turned my mind to work and catching up on emails.

I later overheard a conversation from the young man who had just walked me through the building. He was recounting that his girl-friend's boss just found out today that his headache from the last three months is actually cancer. He will be dead in two weeks or less! She just saw him this morning at work.

She is in shock. Her co-worker is asking her to go with her

to her manager's home to just be with him and his family. She can't bring herself to go as she is so torn up in disbelief!

So I have a choice.

Do I just sit here, or do I *"shout God's goodness from the platform of my trial?"*

I walked over to their table, apologizing for listening in. I softly inserted myself, as God gave me the strength, and shared my Jenny's home going. I shared my faith that has enabled and strengthened me.

I reflected that prior to Jenny's home going I was exactly like him, not knowing what to say when I heard, or saw, others in pain. How could my words or processes be of any help?

I asked the young man about his girlfriend's faith. He told me that she was a person of faith, so I encouraged Him to remind her of the truth found only in God's word. I then told him to encourage her to share that truth with her manager so that he can find comfort.

His manager immediately shared how true this was! He said that he found comfort in God's truth when his dear seventeen year old daughter was in a car wreck, and had since been in a coma for the past eight years. My heart broke as I remarked on the pain he must feel from such a long trial, and the strength he found in Christ to continue on as he has!

What a platform God has given me! I stand in awe of His enablement and cry out for strength to continue to share His goodness.

It was a rather long day that was capped with dinner with several guys from my client's team who were also at this building.

The evening finished with a call from my sister, Isabella. I got to hear of God's providence in her life as she has found an amazing dental practice. She will be joining next Monday. On the call she reminded me of the goodness of God and His strength.

She told me that I needed to encourage my lovely daughters to learn from the godly women who were Jenny's close friends, because I can't be a Mom and a Dad. Let them get that motherly touch and encouragement they need from those ladies. I am to focus on being the Dad God wants me to be.

The tears flow as I thank her for that. I ask that she keep reminding me of these things.

The night finished with a call from Griffin to review a few work items. In closing, I asked him to pray for me on the phone as I was having a tough time.

I am now headed to bed, yearning to have my nightly road call with Jenny to unpack my day and give her my love. The tears flowed as Griffin cried out to God for me, pleading for His grace, strength and comfort!

FRIDAY, JULY 15, 2022

Jenny had such joy in the simple things, in getting things done, adding that perfect touch to every space or finding that perfect deal.

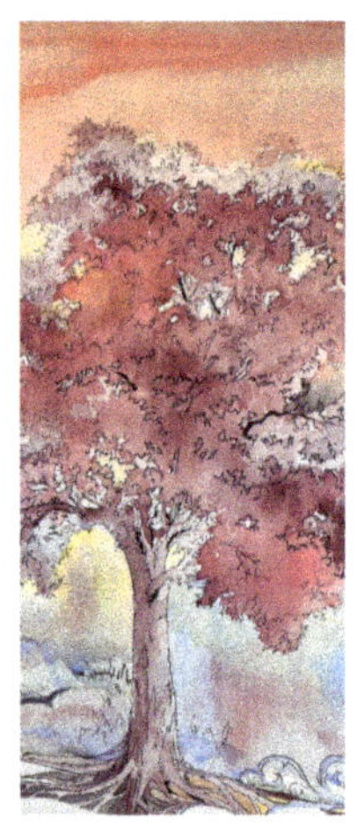

Being on the road this week was a little harder than I anticipated. How I looked forward to that call, before I headed to bed as she shared her day, sending pictures of her terrific finds of furniture—the piece that is now finished ... My heart aches and the tears flow as I reflect on the many calls through the years! I so dearly miss her!

The day was again spent at Ron's new facility. Today there was a lot more sitting and digesting the volumes of information the seller's IT team had handed off. Throughout the day I was able to pause a couple times and check in with Clara and Liz to hear how their days were going, as they navigate their own grief. We celebrated the great sleep God had given us all that night!

Dinner was refreshing as I was with Ron's new COO. He is the gentleman I had gone into the office to meet on the day of Jenny's home going. We spent the meal time with me sharing memories of her, explaining just how much of a help she was to me.

After dinner, I received an encouraging call from my brother in law, Joe. It was so good to hear his voice. As I replayed his call in my head, memories flooded my mind. I see him in my home teaching me how to smoke a prime rib on a charcoal grill. I reflect on his soft tone of encouragement and comfort. I recalled having heard that same tone before as he comforted and encouraged his lovely children. He and Amy are very purposeful parents.

On the call we reflected on the memories that were made just two years ago, when Jesse went to the lake with us and was able to spend quality time with her Aunt Jenny. I treasure those memories!

The night finished with an encouraging call with my brother, Paul, as he reflected on the quote that Anna sent the other day..

"Instead of letting today's hardship come down on top of you, climb on top of it, and shout God's goodness from the platform of your trial"

He remarked about how people think that grief shrinks over time, but that in reality people tend to grow around their grief. He reminded me that if I will continue to be present and be a good listener, I can help others. When we keep quiet and our story runs over and over in our head, it is unhealthy. But when we share our story, it's powerful!

He finished by assuring me that Jenny's memories will not shrink, and that I will grow as I rest in my faith.

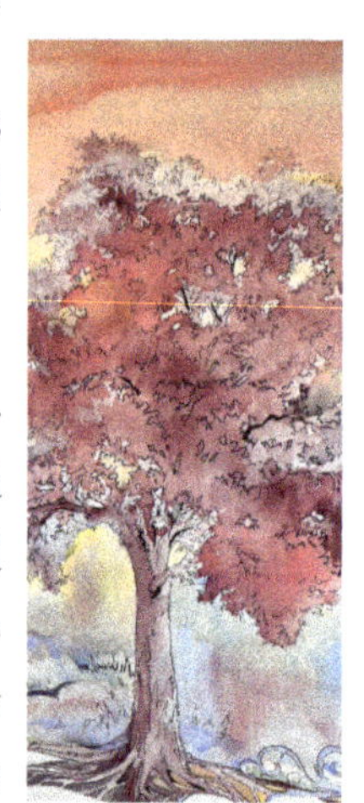

As I reflect on both Paul and Joe's encouragement from yesterday, I am reminded of the mountain of encouraging texts and emails that continue to pour in. I am so grateful for the people God has placed in my life, who call, text, and email me to share their care and comforting words.

I am still in Michigan but heading home today. Ron let me drive and promptly regretted it when I tried to take us through a closed construction area and onto a bridge that was being built! The work crew was in complete shock and disbelief that I made it past all the barriers! After much hand waving and shouts of alarm from the crew, I did a twelve point turn and got us back onto a road that was open.

On the drive home, one memory that Ron recalled was the first Sunday that he and his wife visited our church. She and I sang *Bow the Knee*. His daughters had just sung that same song at a missions conference recently. He also remarked just how grateful he and Stacey were that Jenny invited them to participate in the book study we did last winter—*The Sovereignty of God* by R.C. Sproul.

Ron told me that Jenny's life story, shared over dinner on Tuesday night with his two leaders (Vice President and COO), had made an impact. They both had remarked to him on his morning call with them that they couldn't wait to get home to hug their wives tighter! They were challenged by the way I expressed my love for Jenny.

I arrived home just in time to eat dinner with Luke and Clara. I was covered with a thousand puppy kisses when my puppy girls met me at the door. For dessert, we drove to Chick- fil-A and had an ice cream cone.

When Luke and Clara left, I decided to see if I could find all Jenny's notes and cards. I sat at the counter and read them. Tears flowed as I read her endearing, loving words! I have more at the office and can't wait to read those as well. I am so very grateful that God gave her to me for as long as He did. I pray that I might go out and glorify Him in the same ways that she did!

I pray that Christ will draw me closer to Him so that I might be comforted, strengthened and reflect His love and kindness to others He brings into my path.

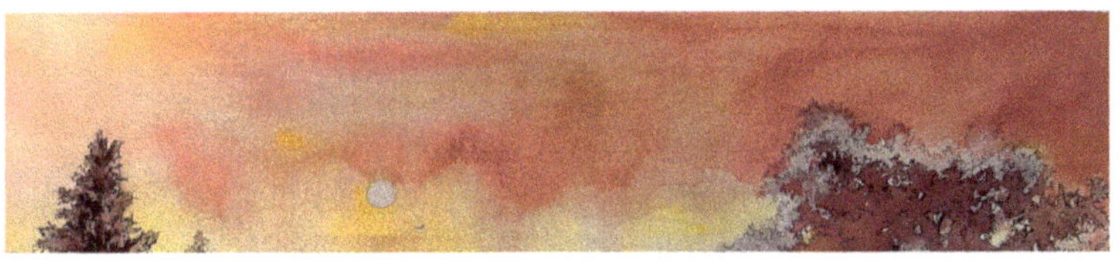

SATURDAY, JULY 16, 2022

I started my morning by reviewing the first three verses of Psalm 34. I have been working on memorizing them so that I might meditate on these truths throughout the day. This Psalm has been such an encouragement to me!

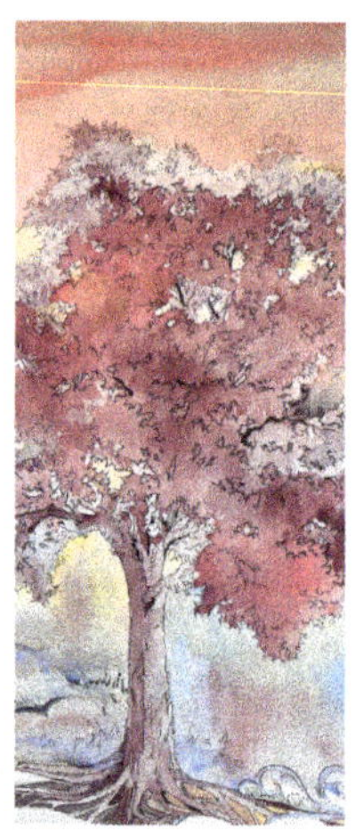

After breakfast, I imagined what she would say today—the task list she would have given me on Friday to make sure I knew what Saturday's priorities were. At the top of the list would have been to pull the weeds in all the beds. Some had become small trees!

The puppies joined me outside. I played my *Sovereign Grace* music and began a sweat fest for the next two hours! I made my way around the pool, then to the back of the house and finally to the front beds.

The day flew by fast. Luke and Clara came over to drop off furniture and eat lunch. When they left, I took a nap out on the screened in porch with the puppies nearby.

Liz had texted earlier telling me that today was Zucchini Bread Day! So I am looking forward to them coming by later.

I ran and got a haircut mid afternoon. On the way there, dinner plans developed, so now I am looking forward to a great night out with the girls and their husbands!

I am so grateful for the stream of texts that continue to pour in throughout each day—they are so encouraging!

As we arrived for dinner and awaited seating, my sister, Isabella, called with words of comfort and encouragement. At dinner, our conversation purposefully focussed on the gift that God gave us in Jenny, who was an amazing wife and mother.

I began by asking what was the biggest hole they now experienced in their lives because of her absence. Both Liz and Clara remarked on the texts or calls spontaneously sent to get their mother's view on something.

I remarked on the role Jenny played in what I wanted to do, when my ideas were not fully thought out or poor in timing. She helped me see its unintended impact. It might fall in a *"not now,"* or *"to be reviewed again in the future"* category. I told them how great-full I was for the grace they had been showing me. I had already thrown out some rash ideas that Liz and Clara graciously navigated to *"let's circle back to that in a few weeks."*

Everyone now has a front row seat to the act now— unfiltered, untethered David!

Jenny did such a good job of balancing me out. And what's even more amazing is that she never gave up! God gave her much grace to stick with me even though I made so many mistakes, leaving her very frustrated so many times.

At dinner we also discussed the need for us all to partner together to remind each other of those days that lie before us—those firsts that are so painful—the first time at church on a Wednesday night or a business trip away...!

I went on to explain that if we think ahead to those firsts, then we can talk about them. Even more importantly, Noah and Luke can bring those into their daily prayers with the girls. Pleading with God for grace in the upcoming circumstance, would remind us all that God is here with us to strengthen us, if we will but ask.

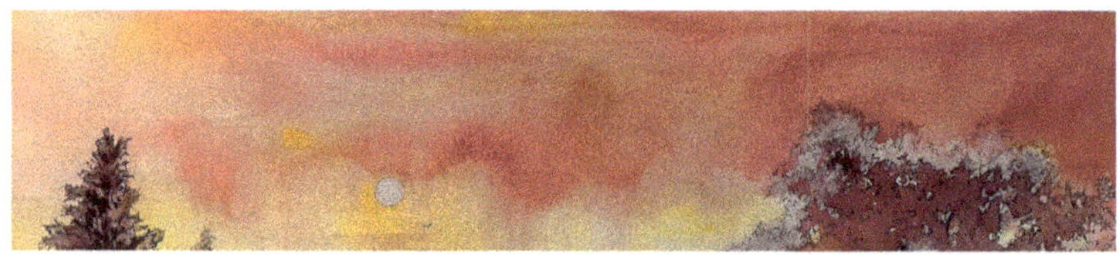

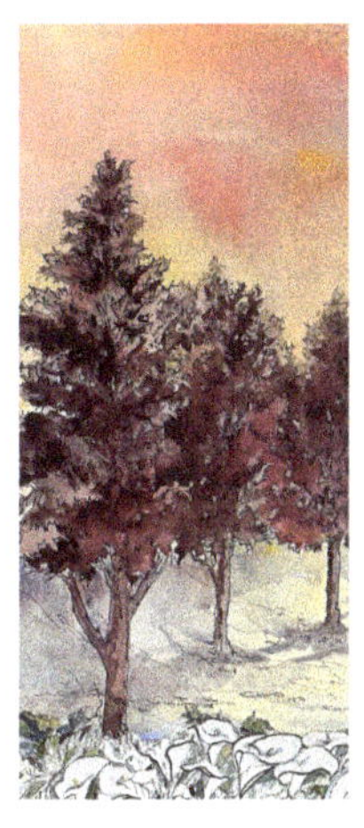

At dinner I reflected on my week on the road. I shared how it was harder than I had anticipated with many more tears. But God was faithful and I was encouraged and comforted.

The night ended back at my house where we enjoyed Liz's Zucchini Bread. It was AMAZING! Perfect taste, texture and temperature—a great blend of textures with walnuts, the gleaming top crust and the soft bounce of the bread with its layers of chocolate chips. I gently spread on a few pats of butter and watched it quickly melt in!

Friday night was my first night back in my bed.

This morning I woke at 6:30 a.m., which means I got eight hours of sleep!

I continue to pray for grace and strength and that God will continue to draw me to Himself so that I might better serve Him and others!

SUNDAY, JULY 17, 2022

This morning I decided to watch the funeral service again. I find that it is very comforting to hear people talk about my Jenny. It evokes so many great memories that I cherish dearly.

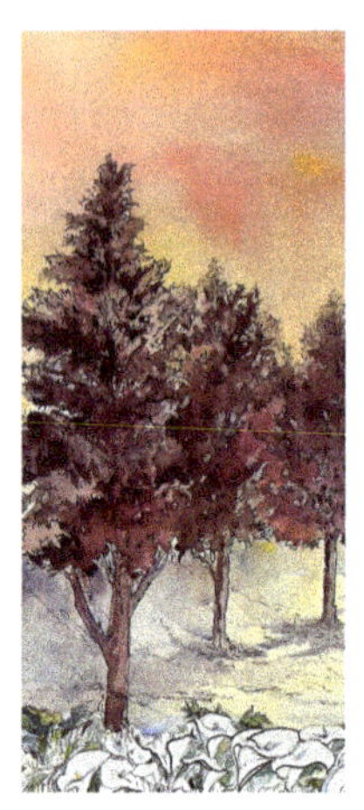

Time slipped away from me and I rushed to get out the door at 9:45, just in time to have a few conversations before being seated! The first person to greet me was Phil Allen—the missionary to New Guiana, who lost his son to a rip tide in Pensacola many years ago.

"How are you really doing?" he asks.

I told him it had been a tougher week than I thought it would be. He commented how the first year is filled with many waves to navigate, as many cherished times will come and Jenny will not be there.

Writing what I just wrote and seeing it in black and white hurts so much, yet I know that Christ will hold me fast. The tears will flow.

The first few songs of the song service were a bit tough as the words washed over my mind and heart. I recalled Jenny pulsing my hand as the words would roll onto the screen.

As Pastor spoke, I was refreshed. I could vividly recall Jenny's passion for God's word and His truth. She was in awe of the fact that a holy and just God would still love her, even though she continued to sin. I think that is why she was so faithful to remind us that we are sinners, and that our sin is no different from anyone else's. She treasured her relationship with Christ and was comforted.

After service, I sat down in Pastor's office as he wanted to share an update on Jenny's memorial fund that will be used for a scholarship. I was humbled and brought to tears when he told me that the donations totaled $22,000!

He printed off all the notes from those who donated. There were even more dona-tions that didn't have a note!

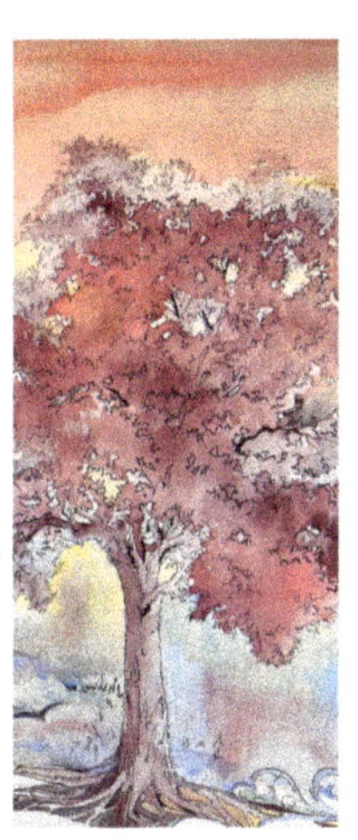

We then shared many tears as he reflected on his memories of her. His office was right next to Jenny's so they had many hours of conversation, either in the doorway of his office or in her office. She was the church secretary and Pastor's wife, Olivia, was the school secretary. They spent countless hours together.

There are so many memories in the church and school. There is not a hall or room she has not been in, not a place where she did not engage in deep conversations, or mark with her special decorating touch.

After church was over and the dogs taken out, I had to run over to my office to get it all cleaned up and organized. I wanted to find my favorite Valentine note that Jenny made me a couple years ago. It's just a simple piece of paper where she expressed her love by using Candy Hearts that have writ-ing on them. Four boxes of trash later, I found it!

When I got back home I decided to get out all our photo albums. I went through them, pulling out all the pictures of my Jenny. I am leaving several more albums out on the table so I have ready access to them. Her smile! And her eyes! She had such joy to overflowing!

As I go to bed, I remind myself of Psalm 34. I have memorized 1-3 and today I started working on 4-6

> *4 - I sought the Lord and He answered me,*
> *And rescued me from all my fears.*
> *5 - They looked to Him and were radiant,*
> *And their faces will never be ashamed.*
> *6 - This wretched man cried out, and the Lord heard him,*
> *And saved him out of all his troubles."*

I can't do this. I need His strength.

I pray that I rest in Christ. May I allow Him to strengthen me and draw me closer to Him.

16

Craig & Rachel

SARA

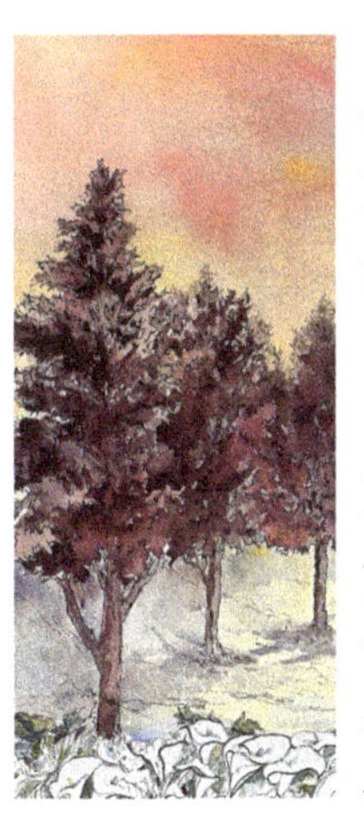

Like Jenny, I never met Rachel's husband, Craig. She spoke to me about him, but I learned the most from the tributes offered by family and friends at his home-going service.

In many churches the title of "Worship Leader" is a paid position and considered part of the essential leadership of the church. Craig served God with his considerable talent for eight years as a Worship Leader. His unbending stipulation was that he would only do so if he was never paid, but considered a volunteer!

He was described as *"unflappable, pastoral and wise, with*

an easy sense of humor." An example of that humor is best described in an incident where one of his friends accidentally killed a deer with his car on a rural road. Since then, Craig would send him text messages with venison recipes every time he thought of him!

Society no longer places value on a biblical family or their individual roles as described by God. Role models for sound marriages are precious and necessary for every generation of believers. In an age where even gender is questioned, the priceless witness of a biblical marriage can never be overstated.

Seasoned married couples quietly influenced me when I was a young wife. That was a long time ago. I would observe their interactions, watching with curiosity to see how minor conflicts and annoyances were handled. Whenever I witnessed love and honor between couples who had been married for decades, it niggled my conscience about being kinder to my husband. A strong marriage is a testimony of unity, forged by purposes greater than individual desires and objectives, clarified in the crucible of life's trials.

Of course, there is much that goes on behind closed doors that none of us are privy to. However, in the best marriages the little acts of grace demonstrated in public are a visible overflow of the love nurtured in the privacy of the union. There is a public view that cannot be hidden, be it of love or of strife. Out of the abundance of whatever is cultivated, the world will glimpse the state of the marriage.

For a watching world, truths about successful marriages are absorbed by observation rather than from class lectures. Craig's pastor co-led a small group of young couples with Craig and Rachel for three years. In his tribute he said that this couple modeled in their marriage all that he was attempting to teach from the Bible in words.

One of his friends, when compiling a devotional for men, asked Craig to contribute his insight on fatherhood. His thoughts below give us the clearest sense of the man, who was Rachel's beloved husband and the father of two respectful teenagers. That his template was drawn from the Bible is apparent in the words of his submission.

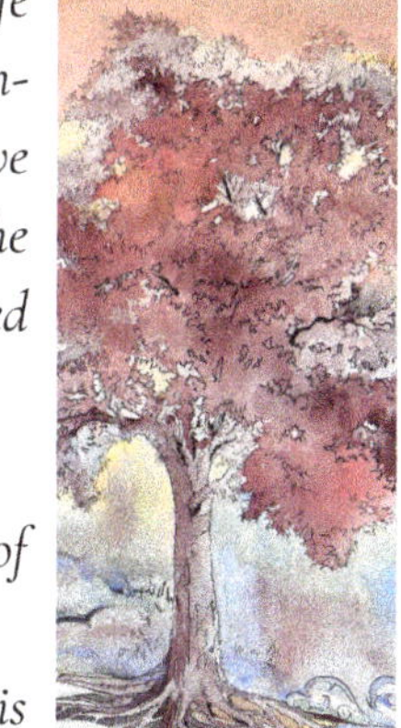

"Becoming a father was one of those life changing events which influenced me, and continues to shape me. It gave me a new perspective of God as my heavenly Father. It changed the way that I read scripture passages that referenced God as my Father.

For example, consider the familiar lines of John 3:16,

"For God so loved the world that He gave His only son, that whoever believes in Him should not perish but have eternal life."

I knew that love motivated God to send Jesus to die for my sins, however, it wasn't until I became a father that the weight of the phrase "His own son" landed on me! I cannot imagine sending my children somewhere to die for anyone—period. The fact that God did that for me, a sinner, is truly amazing, incredible and unbelievable!

When my children want something, they are not afraid to ask. As their father, I love to meet their needs and even their "wants," to give them whatever they ask for whenever I can. God is the giver of good gifts.

These truths about God, my heavenly Father, have become more real to me recently. He loves me and just wants to spend more time with me—no strings attached, just as I do with my children.

We've made lots of memories on family vacations or other great adventures, but I also enjoy just being around my children, spending time with them on the couch after a long week, or singing along with songs on the radio in the car.

Can you relate to this verse as a father?

"He will rejoice over you with gladness,
He will quiet you with His love,
He will rejoice over you with singing." Zephaniah 3:17

Don't you just enjoy being around your children? Do you love to brag about them? When those feelings of satisfaction, pride, and joy well up in you, remind yourself that God, your Father, feels the same way about you.

The next time you come across a passage referring to God, the Father, in the Scripture, I hope that your own experience as a father will provide you a new lens, through which you can view His love for you."

Craig enjoyed his father-daughter retreats with Emma and loved hunting turkeys with Levi.

There was nothing he desired more for them than that they would get to know Jesus intimately as he did. That desire formed the content of his fervent prayers for them, as their earthly father, before he departed.

Their heavenly Father will now faithfully answer those prayers by revealing more of His gracious nature to them. He will walk them through their loss and into a good future that still awaits them.

One day, He will draw them also into their heavenly home where their earthly father, Craig, will greet them with great joy!

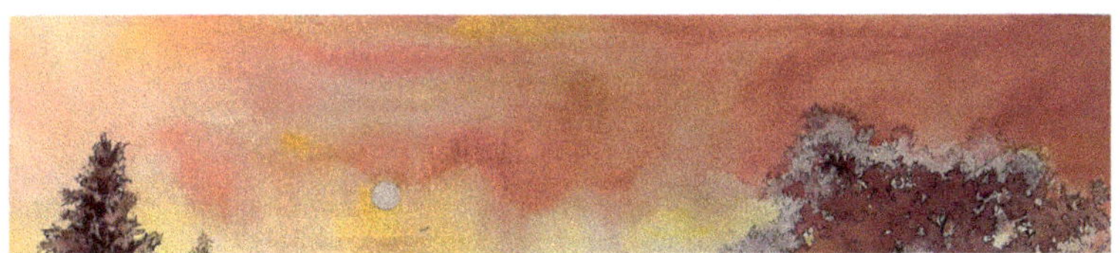

17

❧

God's Gift of Laura

DAVID: MONDAY, JULY 11. 2022

Today is the BIG day that Jenny had dreamed about for the past many months! The baby reveal!

My heart rejoices as I consider how excited she would have been, her big smile, as she would have laid out her clothes for the party later this afternoon.

The night before at the pool, I encouraged Clara to embrace this gender reveal party. I encouraged her to rejoice and sorrow. I told her to not try to stay strong—let the tears flow. We would all be right there, rejoicing and crying with her.

Pastor's message yesterday was about how *"Sorrow forces us to consider what matters and is of most consequence!"*

He walked us through two undeniable realities:

- Life is short, death comes for all
- Eternity is forever

He then offered three Christian responses:

- We should be cultivating a holy dissatisfaction with this world
- Surround ourselves with those who are strong in faith where we are weak
- Jesus is the all consuming treasure of this life

> *"But what things were gain to me,*
> *those I counted loss for Christ."*
> Philippians 3:7 NKJV

After service we returned home to be greeted by an awesome balloon arrangement! Jenny had arranged for some company to deliver this arrangement today. It was sitting there waiting for us when we pulled up—pink and blue balloons, perfectly shaped to help make this day so memorable!

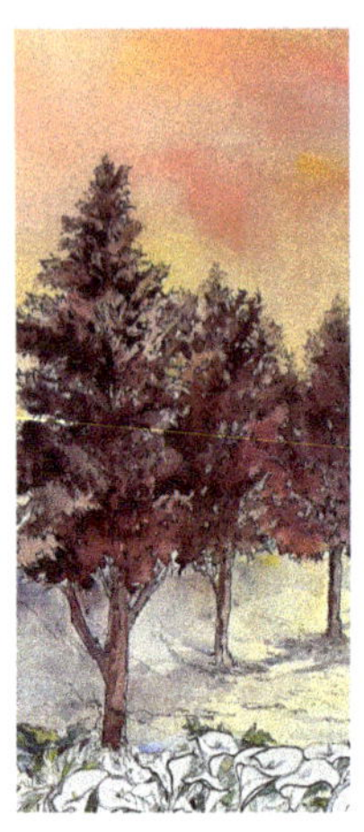

I sat by the grill and watched as so many people worked diligently to make Jenny's dream reveal party come alive. Tables were set with pretty pink and blue table runners. There were those glass mason jars that she so often used, filled with pink and blue colored water with perfect sprays of baby's breath as their crowning jewel!

Every little detail was put in place, and at 4 p.m. the honored guests arrived to eat. The anticipation continued to build towards 5 p.m.—the time of the reveal!

The powder filled balloons and darts were perfectly executed, as Luke and Clara worked their way through the task, taking us down to the wire! Somehow they found three pink balloons and three blue balloons ...and then finally—a fourth PINK one!

I can hear Jenny scream with great joy! And I can see her running over to give Clara the biggest hug ... my eyes fill with tears. What a great day, surrounded by family and friends, as we celebrate the gift of life and a BABY GIRL. I am tickled Pink!

I continue to pray that as I sit in this house of sorrow, reflecting on God's goodness and grace, that He will draw me to Himself.

18

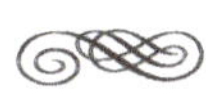

Jenny's Car

Jenny always cared about others.

One memory I treasure is when I tried to honor her. I wanted to show my great appreciation for her love, help, encouragement, and true partnership in my life.

I spent an entire day with her with the goal of getting her a convertible—something just for her to enjoy as she wished. I wanted something significant that represented her significance to me!

The first place we started was at the Lexus dealership. Wow, such a beautiful car—matched well with my ageless

Jenny! She got in, looked in the back seat and remarked that there was not enough room for anyone to sit!

I tell her quickly that it does not matter—this is for her, not for other people.

"You have a passenger seat, you don't need a back seat—this is all about YOU!"

She promptly replied that she will not have something like this that is just for her!

"People must be able to comfortably sit in the back seat. I will not have a car that I can't enjoy with others...We can take Luke and Clara to dinner."

We can ... we can ... other... others ..

There was no further arguing with her. The Lexus was out!

Next, a BMW. The car pulls up, it's amazing looking! The salesman puts the top down and opens the door for Jenny to get in to sit behind the wheel. She immediately asks him how to pull the seat forward so she can sit in the back seat!

He is perplexed, but slides the seat forward. Jenny promptly sits in the back seat and asks him to pull the seat back so she can see what the back feels like!

"Sorry sir, that back seat is not comfortable, way too tight and confined."

She gets out and thanks him for his time.

He wants to talk engineering, performance ...

Me: *"Sorry, the car is for her and she is looking for one that has the best BACK seat! For her it's about her passengers being comfortable!"*

So on to Mercedes, where she finally finds the perfect back seat. Her passengers will be seated comfortably!

"Now I can enjoy it, because others can enjoy it with me!"

That is my lovely Jenny—pulling others into her joy!

19

Sleep

MONDAY, JULY 18, 2022

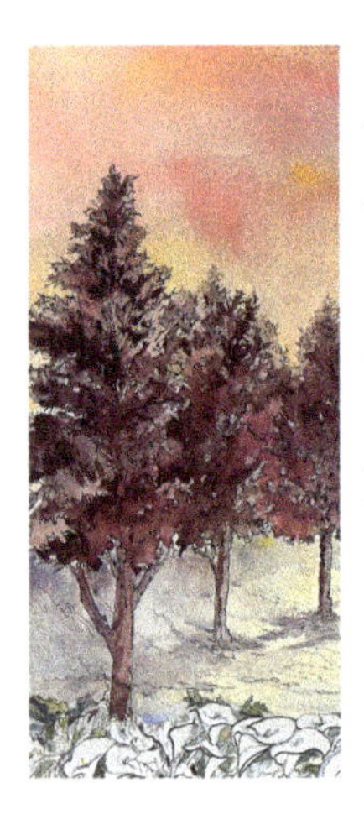

The morning started at 2:30 a.m. I was wide awake and I could not get back to sleep. I decided to watch Jenny's service again. The tears rolled down my face as the song service ministered to my heart. I ended the service with Zoe's remarks about Jenny being her Jonathan—iron sharpening iron, as they challenged each other to learn more of Christ and become more like Him!

By 4 a.m. my eyes finally became heavy again, as I meditated on Psalm 34:1-3, I drifted back to sleep.

I awoke with a vivid dream.

When Jenny was recovering from surgery I told her to wake me up if she was the slightest bit uncomfortable so I could help her move. I would be there to help her, stressing that she must not hesitate to be loud to wake me.

So in my dream I heard Jenny—firmly, with a tremor of pain, *"David … DAVID!"* It was so loud in that I sat up in bed! My heart hurt and the tears returned as I reflected on her pain. It then dawned on me that she will never feel any pain ever again! She is resting perfectly now with Christ, her Lord, and I will see her again!

It's now 5:45 a.m. and time to get the day started for good this time. After my devotions, I scurried about the house making a quick breakfast and coffee. I was on the road to the office by 6:15 a.m. for a 7 a.m. client breakfast meeting. The meeting and morning went along uneventfully. Just before a lunch meeting I was able to sneak in a 2 mile run!

Throughout the day, I continued to meditate on Psalm 34 - playing verse 1-2 over again in my mind.

> *"I will bless the Lord at all times;*
> *His praise shall continually be in my mouth.*
> *2 My soul will make its boast in the Lord;"*

As I headed home for the evening to go to dinner at the Monroe's, I can't get Jenny's home-going service out of my mind. I am in awe of God's grace and strength that He gave me that day. Even more, I see that I am able to function better at work with my mind becoming clearer each day. I can't help but boast and brag about how good He has been to me throughout this trial.

Dinner at the Monroe's was terrific—to see all the family and catch up! The night finished with a delicious triple berry pie that Emily made. While eating, my neighbor from up on the hill, Lisa, called to check on me. She and Donnelly were recovering from Covid, but she wanted to make sure I was Ok. They are so sweet, like an extra set of grandparents.

There is not a day that goes by that I do not receive numerous cards, texts, and calls throughout the day—so many are praying for us all!

Lord, please draw me close and make me of better service to those around me.

WEDNESDAY JULY 20, 2022

Sleep was hard to come by Tuesday night into Wednesday. I was wide awake at 2:30 a.m.—so it's time to start the day. Devotions this morning were focused on the fact that as a believer I am an Ambassador of Christ, which gives me the great privilege of telling others what God has done for me!

As I think about that, my heart bursts to tell how God is sustaining me daily! There is no way I could even roll out of bed and face the day. Yet through His strength, I am able. I see so many around me hurting, in need of the peace and comfort that I have in Christ.

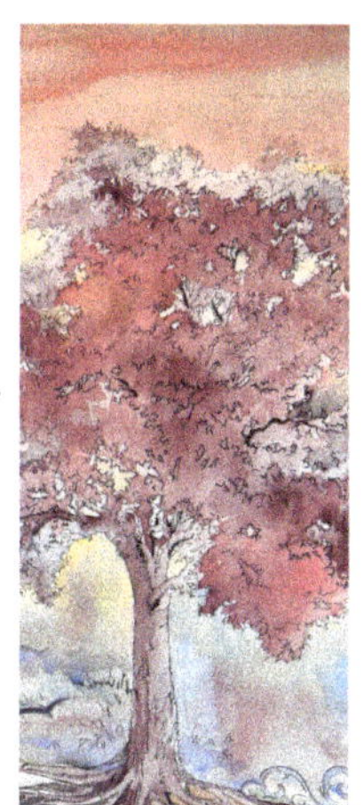

> *"That you may proclaim the excellencies of Him who has called you out of darkness into His marvelous light"* *(1 Pet. 2:9). KJV*

I am in awe of the fact that God knows that I will not live in perfect fellowship with Him. I have taken His grace for granted so many times, yet He still loves me. He calls me to come to Him so He can restore our relationship and to receive His enabling strength, grace and comfort.

While on the drive, I listened to a YouTube video. A pastor spoke at length about Job—a man in the Old Testament, who faced grief on a magnitude I can't wrap my mind around! He literally lost everything, except his wife—possessions, all his children, cattle, etc. His wife tells him he should curse God and die.

Job sat in such a deep, dark pit of grief as he cried out

to God. As I think about my loss, it is so much smaller than Job's. I remind myself that he didn't have the written word of God that I have today. What immediate comfort to me are the Words of God!

His truth is informing my emotions.

Job had to wait to hear God speak to him—and wait he did! What strength and resolve he had to glorify Him! He knew God's character, and surely meditated on what he knew of God, from what He had said and done in his life.

That led him to say, *"Yea though He slay me, I will still trust him!"*

In closing, the preacher remarked that *"The instinct of those suffering is to look backwards, and inwards, for an explanation for the "why" question or "What did I do to deserve this?" The Bible, instead, looks forward in hope and seeks explanation not so much in origins, but in goals, not in cause, but in its results. Where you look makes all the difference in how goes it with your soul and whether you waste your suffering, or grow through it."*

As I arrived at the hotel around 7 p.m., my battery was quite dead. I took Tylenol PM to try and help me sleep a little longer. Asleep by 8 p.m., woke up at 3 a.m.

But that is seven hours!

20

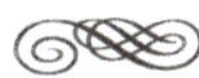

Jenny's Texts

This morning I scrolled through my text conversations with Jenny looking for memories.

I found the following exchange on May the 7th of this year. I was in Pensacola, Florida, visiting my family. I went for a very long run and was passing a memorable landmark familiar to Jenny and me twenty five years earlier, when we were dating.

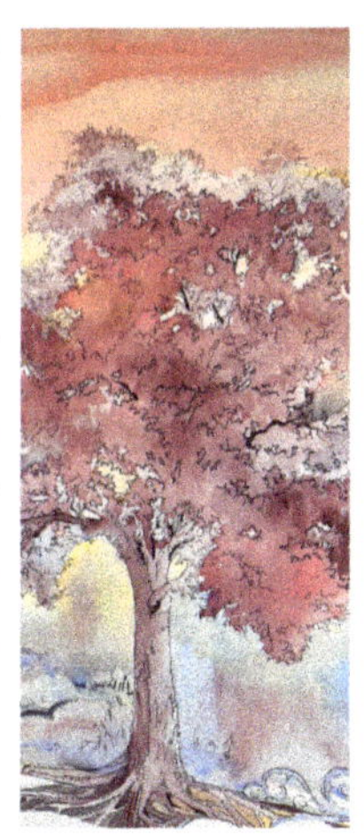

I took some pictures of a building, the parking lot and the intersection, and send it to her. This is the conversation that followed.

Me: *Recognize this parking lot, intersection—9th and Creighton?*

Jenny: *No*

Me: *Sad emoji.*

Me: *It's where this young woman gave me an amazing kiss... Our first kiss!*

Jenny: *Sorry, you know I don't remember locations. I live by my GPS!*

On May 6, there was another memorable text exchange.

Jenny had just texted Clara after Clara had completed her second doctor's appointment for the baby. Jenny forwarded Clara's text to me and was excited to share that she felt strongly that Clara's baby was a girl!

Jenny: *From Clara: The doc's visit went really well! Baby's heart beat was 160 and everything looked good! Just got done about 10 minutes ago, so headed back to the office now.*

Me: *160 is normal, I assume?*

Jenny: *Yes, it is 110-160 in this trimester. Anything over 140 usually/sometimes denotes that it's a girl!*

She was right!

She never did get to meet Laura. They missed each other—one entering, and the other exiting this chaotic world, where time is all too brief.

In eternity, which both will share, time is merely the memory of a concept from their lives on earth—something they will laugh about!

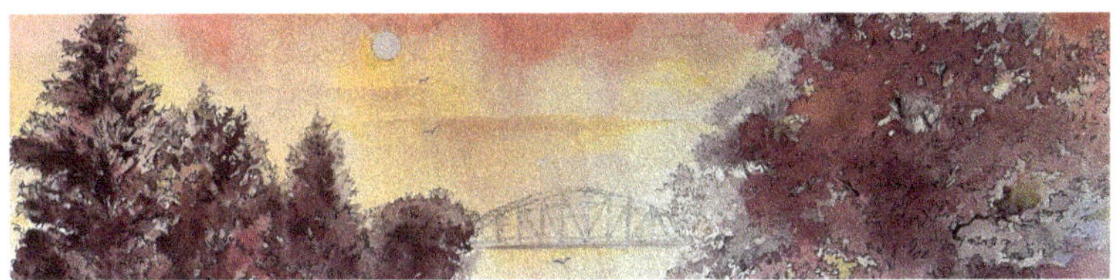

21

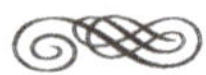

Art is Conversation

SARA

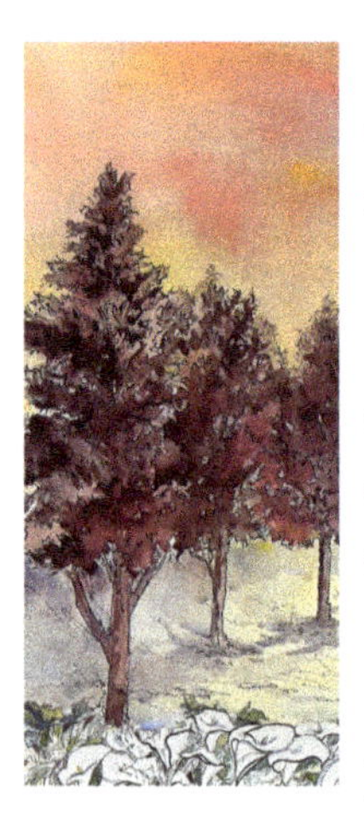

When I created the artwork for David, I did not know him from the journal as you now know him.

It was long after Rachel saw her gift of art, and accepted David's hand in marriage, that the more intimate details of their story were shared with me.

Creating commissioned art for clients begins with minimal knowledge of pertinent facts to be included in the work. Most of their story lies behind the veil of privacy. I ask only as much as is necessary for a suitable idea to capture their aspirations for the work.

This way of working is thrilling to me. Fleshing out the painting is the best part of my adventure with the Lord!

I work in happy ignorance of the nuances of my client's stories and pray that God will reveal interesting facts to build meaning into the artwork. God knows what I need to know and He will tell me, if He feels it is necessary.

Sometimes the things He has told me have taken clients by surprise, since there was no way that I could have known those details about them.

I didn't. God did!

He just chose to tell me to make the work more significant for all of us!

Prayer is the best part of creating art for me! I am, therefore, not as enthusiastic, as I once was, about painting with painting buddies, or painting in front of others in workshops or demonstrations. Art has become such a private activity now, since I maintain a continual conversation with Jesus in my studio.

I ask Him, *"What do I include, what do I leave out? What colors will work with what was shared, what symbols...?"*

He helps me.

I add, remove, add again, and pray some more. Sketches are made and discarded. In the end, the work must be well composed, not a disparate grouping of elements the client insisted on including. Most clients don't quite know what they want, they merely have a faint sense of it.

All elements must work as an aesthetic, cohesive whole that tells their story. They trust my instinct for composition, color, design....even while cherishing their own unique ideas for the artwork. I try to work in that delicate middle ground, trying to find harmony between their desires and the un-explored significance that could yet be included in the work. Those mysterious notes are what I hope to uncover and in-clude in either shapes, colors, symbols or textural elements.

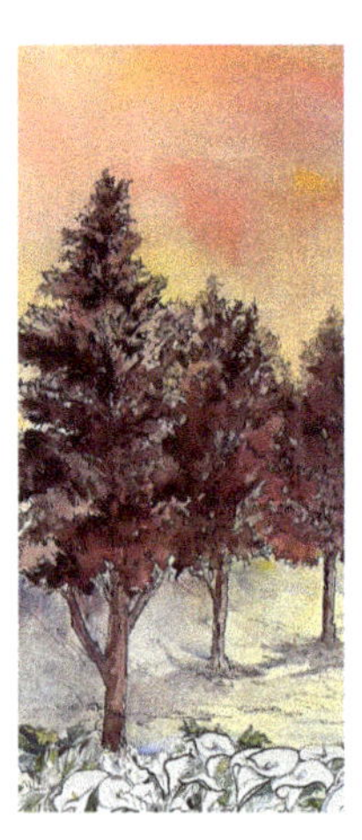

In David's case, I had the added challenge of being in a race against time. The engage-ment was just a week away!

I had to visually communicate their jour-ney this far. But even more, I had to somehow paint their hope for the future without di-minishing all they had already been through.

Needless to say, my response was much like what I read later in David's journal.

"I can't do this without you, Lord!"

Every stroke of the brush is an act of faith. I truly have no idea how the work will turn out or the direction it will take. In the end, I decide I've succeeded if my clients sense in the artwork what they had requested—those specific emotions, ideas and symbols. They are my first audience to please.

Later, I know others will view the work and bring their own interpretations to it, as their unique responses to line, shape and color, will inform their emotions. That is the beautiful quality of art—it speaks, and keeps on speaking—the interpretation of its language being as personal and unique as the one viewing it.

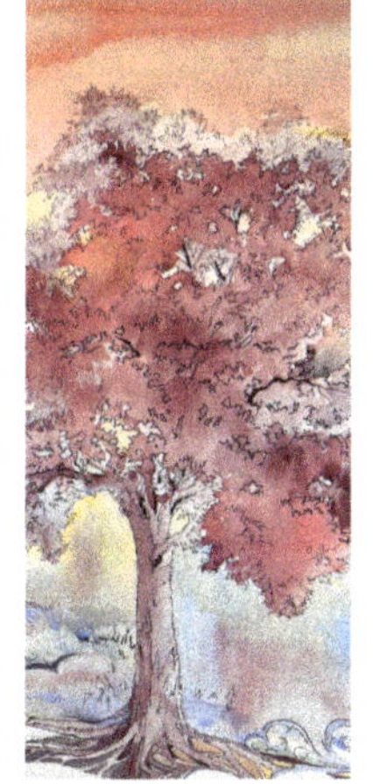

Someone once asked me if I created like Michelangelo created David! Nothing could be more different in my work process. First, it is laughable to include me in the same sentence as that genius of marble. But the one who asked was genuinely perplexed about all artistic processes. For her, all artists may well have been mythical beings. She had not the foggiest idea about how messy creating art is for a lesser mortal like me!

For Michelangelo's sculpture of David, he chose a block of Carrara marble that most sculptors would not have touched, because it was awkwardly proportioned. That is the distinction between a genius and the rest of us. We prefer familiar materials, in proportions with which we have already experienced some measure of success. Of course, as a result we don't create masterpieces—just works of art that some find enjoyable.

As I write this, I remind myself to endure the discomfort of odd proportions, because who knows, it just may result in a masterpiece! I'll add it to my list of things to attempt when life is a tad less hectic.

Seeing Michelangelo's David in Italy took my breath away —literally! I almost expected him to turn his ferocious gaze away from his vision of victory over Goliath to look at me with pity. Towering over me, he was glorious! Michelangelo's handling of marble defied its essential nature as a cold, unyielding stone, transforming it into resembling smooth, rippling, sensuous flesh.

Art historians tell us that when he viewed that awkward piece of stone, Michelangelo envisioned young David trapped in it and simply set him free! The process sounds effortless, and perhaps, for him it was. I can see myself chop away some essential anatomical detail if freeing him was left up to me! Before you get too many funny ideas on how that might have turned out, I'll switch to telling you about my way of working!

I lack the confidence of skill to which I can claim any ownership. If God did not grace me, I could not create—a fact that I am acutely aware of. If I succeed at any work it is because of His anointing for the task. If I fail, it is because I did not quite yield to Him as I ought to have.

So creating a commissioned work of art is a searching, seeking process, as I pray. I draw upon the symbolic, visual vocabulary that has become familiar to me from having worked this way before. Occasionally I'll include a new idea or concept that He just taught me. Using line, shape, color, form and texture, I try to tell the client's story on the surface that I am working on, be it paper, canvas or clay.

While Michelangelo's chisel chipped away excess stone to liberate David from the confines of the block, I use both additive and subtractive actions to tell my story in art. It is similar to the difference between modeling and carving—both are methods for sculpture, yet different in the process. And ultimately, both processes result in art.

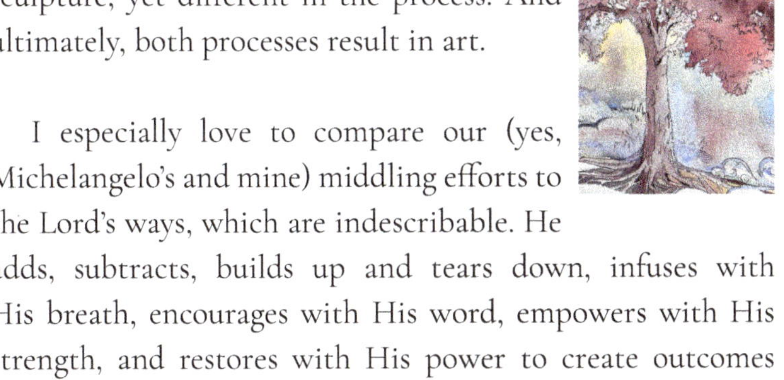

I especially love to compare our (yes, Michelangelo's and mine) middling efforts to the Lord's ways, which are indescribable. He adds, subtracts, builds up and tears down, infuses with His breath, encourages with His word, empowers with His strength, and restores with His power to create outcomes that are beyond compare. To call what He does "art" is to belittle it.

His work is always fresh and ongoing, its final appearance remaining invisible until His scheduled "big reveal" in eternity. This is not an unveiling of any tangible object that man would call a work of art. I am talking about His matchless work in the hearts, minds, and spirits of His children!

22

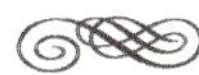

The Gift of Grief

Jenny was in awe of God—that He would love her unconditionally.

How could He, a Holy God, want a REAL relationship with her? She was in awe that she could cry out to Him in grief, pain and sorrow and He would hear her—that He would want to walk with her daily and that she could talk to Him at any time about anything!

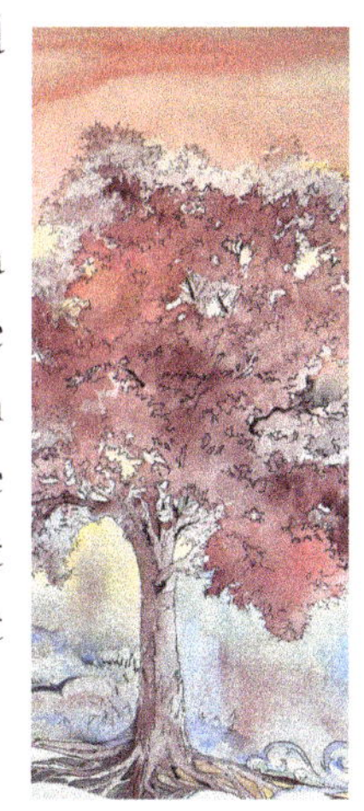

She was on a mission to know more of Him. As she did, she became more like Him.

She was far from perfect. And she knew that, reminding

our family and her friends that sin hurts others, saying, *"I will disappoint, but God will not!"*

Jenny treasured the relationship she had with God. As she navigated her cancer scare, her source of strength and comfort was Christ. She was resting in him and He gave her much grace!

Yesterday the work day went by swiftly, I took a couple power naps to get through the day.

What a gift to be able to work alongside my lovely daughters! I walk across the office, give a quick peck on their foreheads or a good squeeze of the shoulder as I walk to a meeting. Their many visits to my office, their snuggling with the puppies, the priceless conversations about their dear mother—all gifts!

I am in disbelief today! It has almost been a month already! The hole in my life and heart is so very big, but God has given such grace, strength, and continual comfort! Liz and I contemplate this as she snuggles with the puppies! Tears flow and smiles come as we remember...

I had dinner tonight with Liz and Noah. Wow, what tasty bites—a Mexican pasta dish and a great salad! I wonder out loud how much weight Noah has gained since marriage, only to learn he has lost weight because Liz cooks very healthy meals!

Conversation at the table and on the couch is priceless as we marvel at how God is using so many people in our lives to minister grace and truth to us. They are true friends. This is genuine fellowship—walking down the boulder-filled road of grief. Grief is provoking us to godliness! I am encouraged to deepen my relationship with God. I desire to root out sin that is preventing me from being holy and pure like my great God.

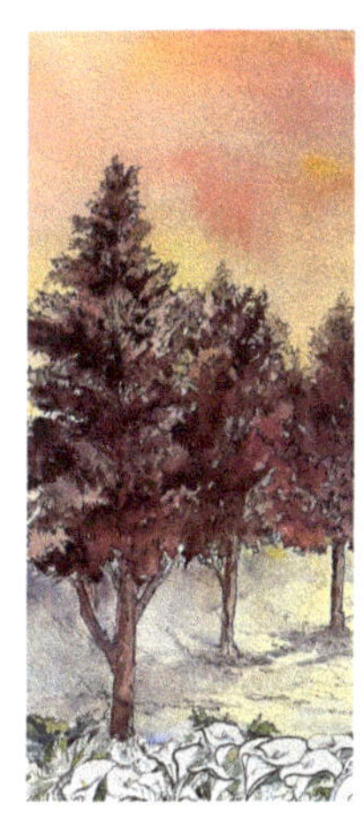

I am so very thankful that God brought Liz and Noah, and Luke and Clara together. I am also so very thankful for this gift of grief so early in their marriage, so that it might propel them to God. It will create a foundation of grace and truth—a marriage that can withstand the tests that will come!

Grief is a gift in my life. It has humbled and propelled me into the arms of a Great God, who through His Spirit has helped me see the ugliness of my sin and my great need for continual dependance on Him.

I can't do this life on my own!

O God, I need you, and you alone! I ask now for your enabling grace so that I might root out sin, honor and glorify you!

23

Jenny Awaits

This morning started at 4:30 a.m. More progress!

As I worked through writing out my reflections in my journal, I was so comforted knowing that Jenny is in the arms of her Savior now. Her race on earth was run well and her life's purpose was completed.

My devotional this morning reflected *"Contemplating your eternal inheritance should give you joy that transcends any temporal circumstance. "*

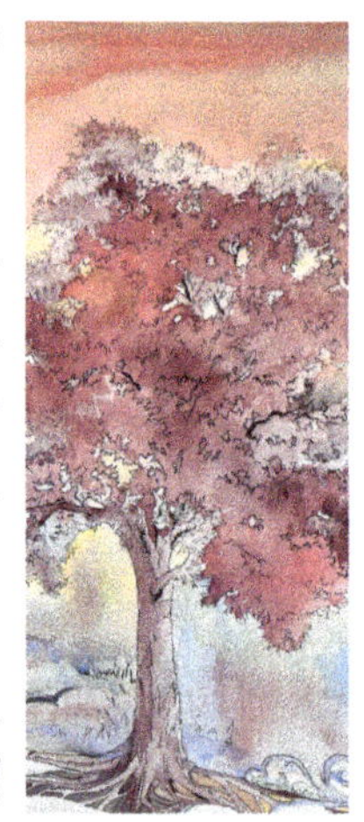

> *"In this you greatly rejoice,*
> *though now for a little while, if need be,*
> *you have been grieved by various trials,"*
> *1 Peter 1:6 NKJV*

As I reflect, I am so thankful that life is so short! This life is only the beginning. My hope and joy is in Christ, the One who created all things and who has promised me an eternal home with Him—where my Jenny awaits.

So what is this "eternal inheritance?"

Hebrews tells us that as a result of Christ's death, *"those who are called may receive the promised eternal inheritance."* It is eternal salvation and eternal redemption.

> *"And having been perfected,*
> *He became the author of eternal salvation*
> *to all who obey Him..."*
> *Hebrews 5:9*

O God, thank you for sending your Son to that "awe-full" cross to bear the weight of all my sins, so that I might have eternal life and an eternal inheritance!

This morning, after devotions I spent more time listening to a book by Elizabeth Elliot.

I can clearly see now that my idea of perfection and joy is very different from God's. I believed the devil's lie that Jesus is not enough. I replaced Him with emotions and feelings that I felt I was entitled to having. I deserve, I want...! I see others have an experience and feel I should be able to have that as well. So when I am unable to experience what I feel I am entitled to, I become upset! This is unfair!

I feel all this because I am looking to those emotions and feelings to satisfy me!

Could grief be classified as a thorn in the flesh?

Could it be that all those emotions, experiences, that satisfaction of closeness that my heart longs for ...could it be that the absence of those longings IS God's grace to me, evoking deep grief, necessary to propel me to Him so that I stop trying to do life in my own strength?

I ask that, and shout a resounding *YES!* That is so true for me! I clearly see now that my dear Jenny's death and my grief is that pulse of pain I needed to thrust me to Him.

I see I can't get out of bed without Him! And yet I valued my desires, my fulfillment and joy over Him. What an amazing gift suffering is to us! It helps us see where our eyes are focused and draws us closer to Him—our chief Joy.

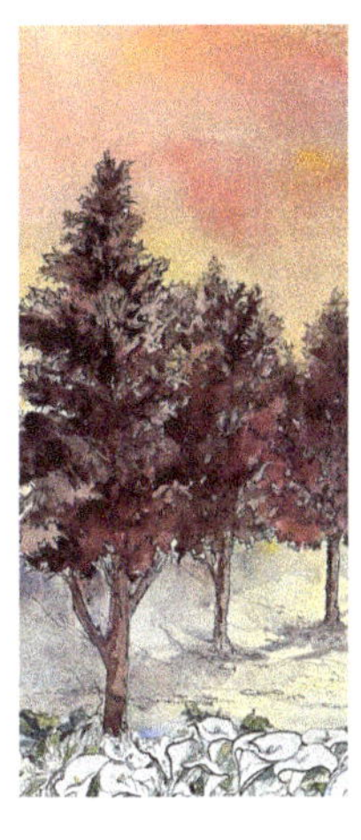

I am in Evansville In this afternoon—big meeting on Wednesday. Steve Graham is in Evansville so I went up tonight to have some quality time with him after work.

What great conversation and fellowship we enjoyed at dinner! We were joined by Nick Johnson and his wife. Nick works with Steve and me and lives in Evansville. Nick's oldest brother died last year. He was in Pensacola and was hit by a truck as he walked along the side of the road.

Over dinner we shared and reflected on great memories of Jenny and Nick's brother, ending the dinner reflecting how God has used our unique griefs in our lives. Steve was grieving the loss of his marriage with his divorce recently finalized.

I am so great-full to God for such close friendships!

O God, I can't do today without you and your strength! I beg you to transform my heart. Give me eyes to see you and your glory. May I look to you for my joy and strength—guide my steps. Keep my eyes and mind fixed on you.

May my actions, and reactions to life today, honor and glorify you. Help me to see each difficulty today as your grace to me —reminding me that you are my true Joy!

24

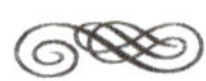

Hearing God

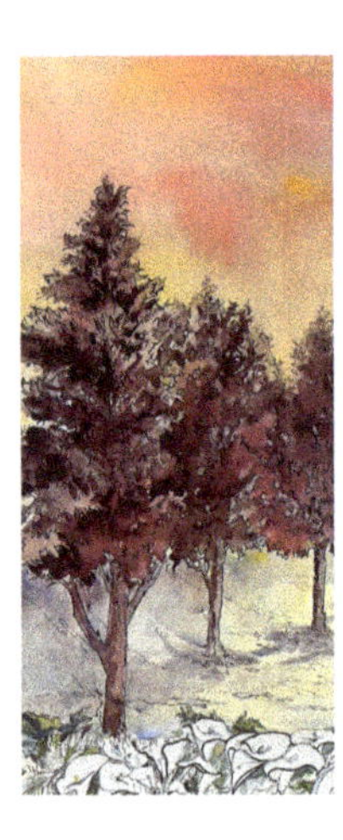

I find myself looking at the dates noted on the top of each photo of Jenny. As I look at these dates, memories flood my mind. The most recent significant event I was great-full for was Jenny's apology to her volleyball team.

During one volleyball tournament she made some coaching decisions that caused significant hurt among several players and ultimately impacted all the players.

I still remember receiving a call from Clara and Luke. They told me just how hurt the players were and asked for counsel about how to handle this with Jenny. They felt they tried to tell her how her decision would cause pain for the team, but wondered what they could have done differently. They wanted to know how they should encourage her to make it right.

I received that call early afternoon on a Saturday. I so clearly recall that evening—Jenny arriving home and over dinner telling me about her day, how it went at the tournament, and then at the hospital with Liz. She remarked, with great heaviness of heart, how her coaching decision had hurt several girls and impacted the entire team. She was grieved that she hadn't seen that it would cause such deep pain for several girls.

Later that evening, when catching up with Luke and Clara, we marveled that God worked in Jenny's heart so rapidly to enable her to see the hurt she caused. She called them, telling them that she was going to make it right. She would sit down and apologize to them individually.

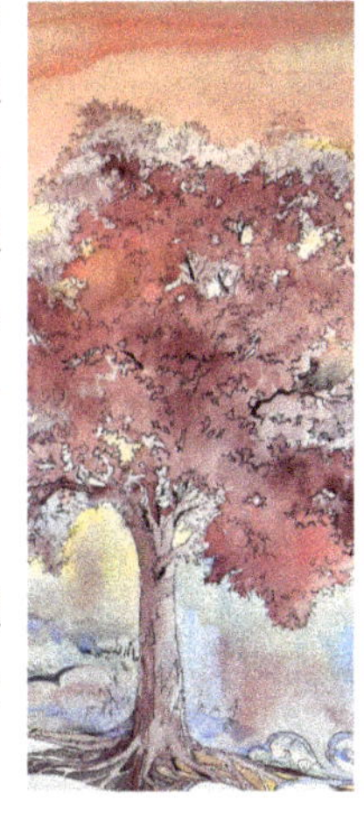

Luke and Clara thought that I had talked to Jenny to help her see how she had hurt the girls. I had not, but God had!

Jenny then deliberately scheduled meetings with each girl. She sat down with them, and their mothers, to hear from them how she had hurt them, and then she apologized!

I am so grateful to God for the transformation I kept seeing in Jenny. I saw God continually changing her so that she became so tender, quickly seeing when, and how, she had unintentionally hurt others.

Once she saw she had, she immediately started the humbling, difficult work of asking for forgiveness to make the relationship right again!

The work day flies by! I am in Evansville all day in client meetings and will hurry back to Louisville, just in time for the retirement dinner party for Quinn Ellis, my CFO.

After dinner, I hurried home to see my fluffy puppies, who covered me with puppy kisses. Once settled in, I finished my book on suffering by Elizabeth Elliot.

As soon as I finished I could feel the heaviness of sleep setting in. I wanted to go to bed right away. Yet, I continued to toy with a thought from the book that I just couldn't shake loose!

Every little unmet expectation I have, every ache, pain, disruption to my plan... are all God's gifts of grace to me to help me discern where I am seeking joy and fulfillment. So, as I am tired and heading to bed, this key thought plays through my mind.

Am I going to accept these as gifts with gratitude?

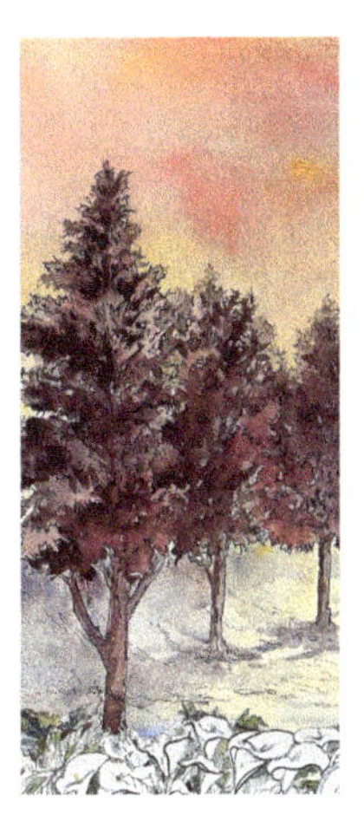

I get the house all shut down and breakfast set up for the morning. As I crawl into bed, Hazel decides she suddenly needs to pee! What? Come on! I thought you just went!

"But Dad, I just need to pee...pretty please?"

I am so aggravated, I should be asleep already! Why now?

I hustle her to the door in a hurry. As I reach the door, it's like God says to me,

"See, there are so many little events in your day you want to control. As soon as your plan is disrupted, you get upset!

You keep begging me to help you and I keep trying to. I give you these gifts of grace, throughout the day, to remind you that you need Me.

It is a reminder to keep your eyes fixed on Me, to be content and to express continual gratitude, but you keep seeing them as rude interruptions to your plan for the day!"

I walk out the door with Hazel, saying,

"O God Thank You for showing me this. Please continue to transform me. I need your help! Help me see daily interruptions as your gifts of grace, meant to remind me of my need for you.

Remind me to keep my eyes fixed on you for my source of joy, comfort and strength!"

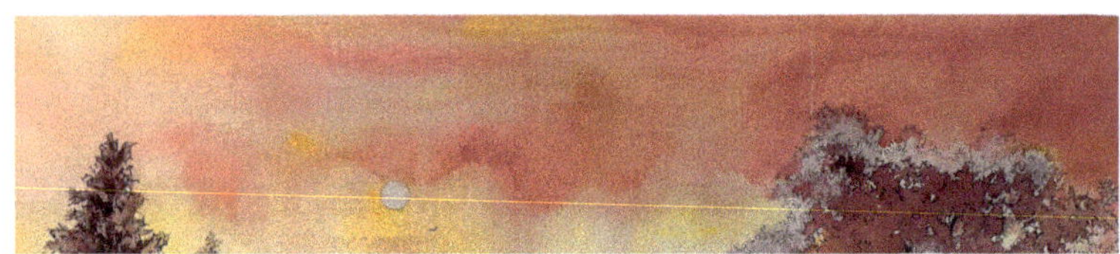

25

Rachel

Fear can choke life.

Rachel's words at Craig's home-going service hinted at the fears she would soon have to face—alone. She now keenly felt the unfamiliarity of his absence, like an amputee who just lost a limb. He was her rock, her anchor, her steady source of comfort in their journey through life. Suddenly she was trapped in a stifling state of loneliness.

In this fallen world losing a loved one is inescapable. People enter and leave earth at a pace that is staggering. Birth and death announcements pound like twin beats on the same drum.

God is the only certain source of comfort, who remains long after other comforters have returned to their own lives. The widow and the fatherless hold a special place in His heart for He is aware that they have lost the protective covering of the man of the house. He steps into their lives as their Father, if invited. If not, He still watches over them without intruding on their autonomy, looking for whenever that entry may be freely granted.

Widows are uniquely vulnerable. Life continues to swirl around them, uncaring of their sudden loss. After offering condolences and some comfort, people move on with their busy lives. Widows are then left with the reality, which only intensifies with time, that their lives will never ever be the same again.

> *"A father of the fatherless,*
> *and a judge of the widows,*
> *is God in his holy habitation."*
> Psalm 68:5 KJV

Even when the nation of Israel, after ignoring innumerable pleas to obey, was eventually judged, His wrath did not extend to the widows or the orphans. He preserved them with tender compassion.

> *"Leave thy fatherless children,*
> *I will preserve them alive;*
> *and let thy widows trust in me."*
> Jeremiah 49:11 KJV

In loss, He can be trusted to be a better husband than earthly husbands could ever be. However, He does require faith in the midst of the trials of every day living. He promises to protect and provide for their needs, but they must believe Him, ask and avail of His goodness in faith.

Then He uses His people to serve their needs by reminding them to be mindful of those in their midst who are vulnerable, widows like Rachel.

> *"Pure religion and undefiled*
> *before God and the Father is this,*
> *To visit the fatherless and widows*
> *in their affliction,*
> *and to keep himself*
> *unspotted from the world."*
> James 1:27 KJV

His expectation is that, in return, widows will remain

faithful to Him and maintain their purity in their singleness. Younger widows were expected to return to a state of marriage once again in purity.

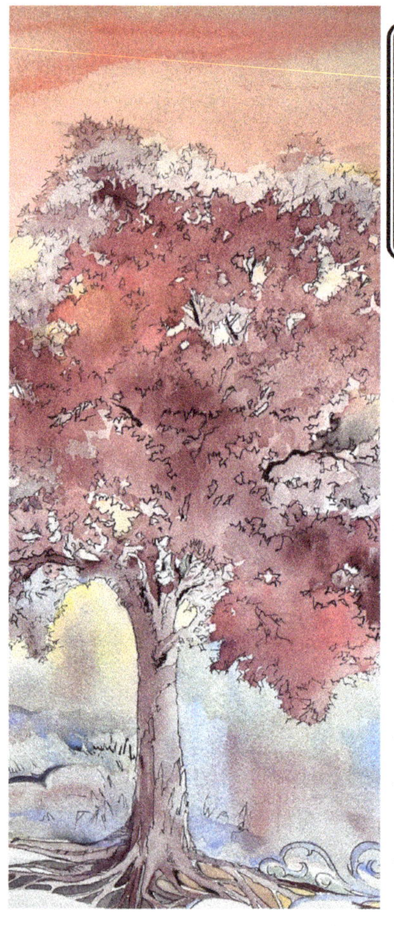

> "Honour widows
> that are widows
> indeed."
> 1Ti 5:3 KJV

Rachel had many favorite verses that she rehearsed often at difficult times in her season of widowhood, never realizing that soon she would be a bride again.

As she honored God by trusting Him, He blessed her with another husband in David. Verses from Luke were among those which offered her comfort, when she struggled with concern about her future.

"Consider the lilies how they grow:
they toil not, they spin not;
and yet I say unto you,
that Solomon in all his glory
was not arrayed like one of these.
If then God so clothe the grass,
which is today in the field,
and tomorrow is cast into the oven;
how much more will he clothe you,
O ye of little faith?

And seek not ye what ye shall eat,
or what ye shall drink,
neither be ye of doubtful mind.
For all these things
do the nations of the world seek after:
and your Father knows that ye have need
of these things.
But rather seek ye the kingdom of God;
and all these things
shall be added unto you."
Luke 12:27-31 KJV

Rachel's verses of comfort are also seared in my own spirit. In partnership with the Lord, I published an adult devotional coloring book that focussed on these very words. Its pages were filled with ink drawings of different kinds of lilies to color meditatively. The curvy, organic shapes of the lilies became familiar to me in that hectic season of creativity leading to its publication and distribution.

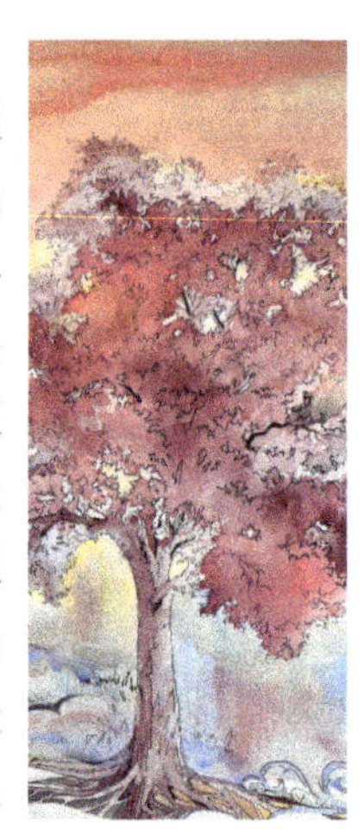

Many wrote to me from around the world about the hope that soaked into their spirits erasing anxiety, as they colored and meditated on these verses. It is such a simple activity—coloring like little children, and trusting God just like them. And yet it brought adult benefits, because God's word is so powerful. As each entrusted their cares to God, He faithfully did the hard work of caring, providing and protecting them in their harsh, grownup world.

I heard of one book that was gifted to a loved one in prison. Unfortunately, there were many men in that cell and a single book was insufficient to meet their need for comfort. So pages were ripped out and shared! I heard that another book was traded for ten cans of soup!

The books were merely the means to draw rough, broken men to Jesus, who was more than able to fill their emptiness with hope. I never cease to marvel at the power of God's word!

Led by the Spirit, I included a swath of voluptuous calla lilies with a dense clump of their fleshy leaves in the foreground of Rachel's painting. It was only later that I heard of her fondness for Jesus' words that instruct us all to *"Consider the lilies..."*

I pray that that little detail will always serve as a reminder to her of God, who more than met her many desperate needs in her darkest hours. I think then of others who will view the art in the new home that David and Rachel are now building together.

May the art also prompt them to turn their anxieties over to Jesus, as they *"Consider the Lilies..."* as He instructs us.

Generations to come will still need to be taught that His words are timeless and He never changes. Perhaps the art will last for yet another generation?

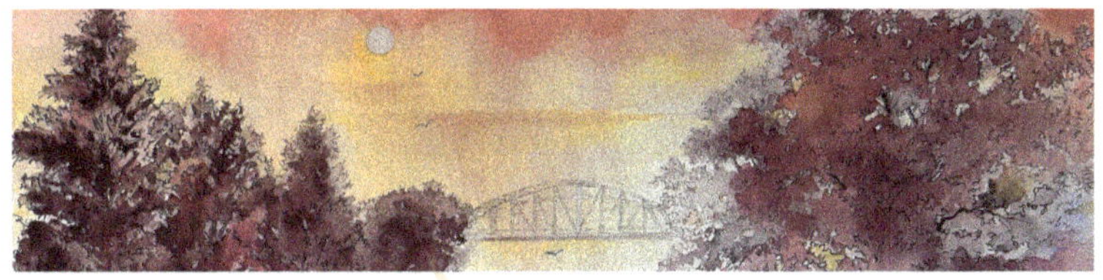

26

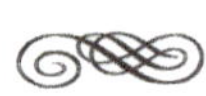

Is That Art?

Rachel called to thank me for the art after David's carefully planned proposal in the Louisville Waterfront Park.

A prominent bridge on those grounds spans the Ohio River and connects Louisville to Jeffersonville, Indiana. She and David spent many hours together in deep conversation walking on that iconic bridge. They had once been high school friends, before college and their marriages took them down different paths.

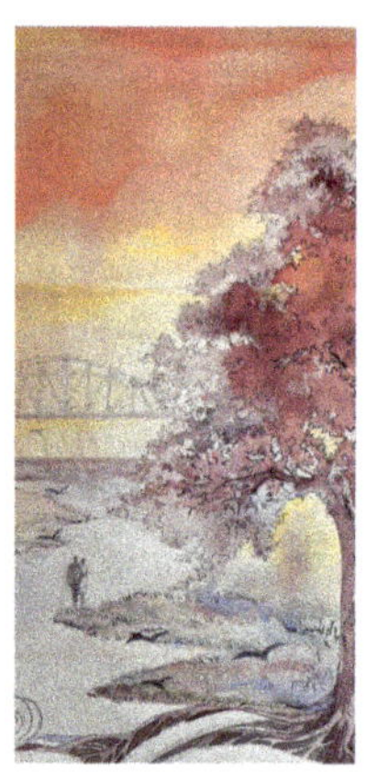

When David lost Jenny, Rachel found out about it and reached out. She had her experience of the faithfulness of God through her widowhood to share with him. The tapestry of their lives carried the common somber strands of grief and faith.

It was the Lord, who wove the shimmering golden thread of love to bind their season of sadness to a close with finality.

The spectacular water views from the Louisville Bridge of the Ohio River formed the backdrop for David's proposal and the landscape for the art. He was getting engaged and he wanted it to be wonderful!

The artist in David envisioned every detail of the proposal. What he would say, when he would ask for her hand in marriage, when the photo of the art would be handed to her... The executive in him made sure that events unfolded exactly as planned.

I had been instructed to somehow include that bridge in the art. I thanked God for the internet, which supplied me with plenty of views of the bridge, the park or any other detail of the surroundings that merely sparked my curiosity.

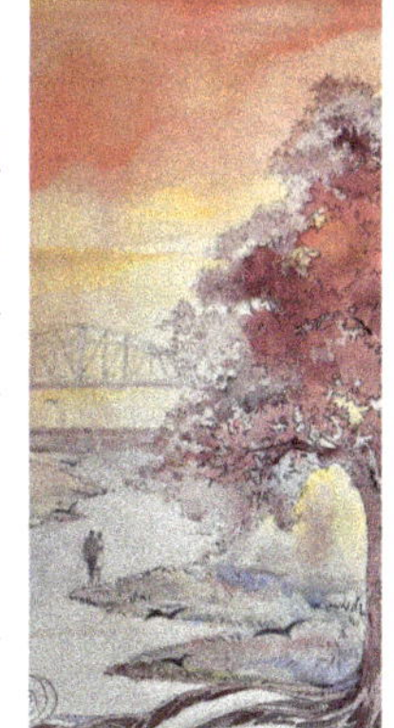

He didn't care if the bridge was only faintly in the distance, he wanted it included. The smallest hint of it would remind them of this unexpected, and holy, season.

He said that it felt like they were standing in the painting as this momentous event of his life unfolded! After he proposed, he handed her the beautifully printed copy of the art that would be shipped later.

I never dreamed that my work could elicit such strong emotions without ever having visited this specific location or met these two, whose lives were being knit together by the Lord. Such are His strange and wonderful ways of working! I was an invisible presence at the event, grateful to be included with His gift of art, wrought with my messy toolkit of paints, inks, brushes and paper.

In the painting, the bridge floats in the distance over the landscape. From the chaos of its interconnecting steel trusses, the morning light quietly glints off one truss that is shaped like a cross—a visible reminder of Jesus, without whom this union would never have occurred. That cross spoke volumes for the journey that was already behind them and exemplified the hope yet ahead.

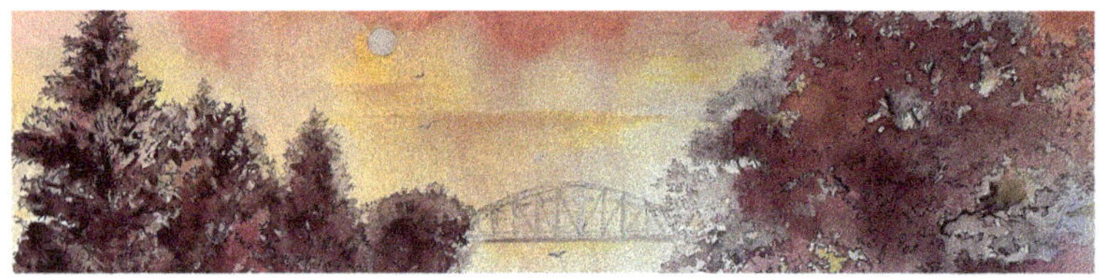

Only Jesus can bridge chasms of differences between two who come together in marriage. Only He knows the baggage from the past that we are helpless to be rid of. He alone understands disparities in heritage, culture, life-shaping childhood events...

Even aspects of good qualities that two possess require uniting in marriages. God's supernatural work of smoothing out raw edges, to neuter their destructive potential, is desperately needed for every union. Marriage was His idea and He doesn't take too kindly to variations from His original intention.

> *"For this reason a man shall leave*
> *his father and mother*
> *and be joined to his wife,*
> *and the two shall become one flesh*
> *So then, they are no longer two*
> *but one flesh.*
> *Therefore what God has joined together,*
> *let not man separate."*
> Matthew 19:5-6 KJV

Although two become one flesh, their spirits remain independent. Two distinctly different spirits can only remain in a harmonious union if they are yielded to the third Spirit, who unites them, the Holy Spirit of Jesus—another reflection of the genius of God. We are utterly helpless without Him!

I got to know David a little from our many interactions over a brief, hectic week to create the painting. Rachel, however, remained a mystery to me until after the commission was completed. His passion for art was evident in the free flow of ideas given to me for the finished product.

But how about Rachel? Did she care about art? He assured me that she would love the idea of this gift. It was only later that I learned about her husband, Craig's, link to art.

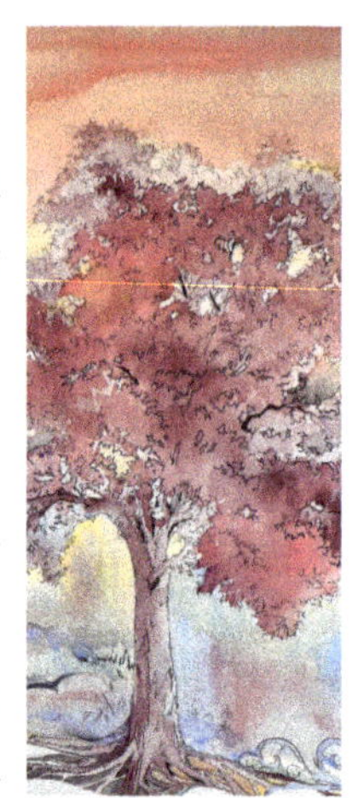

As David and Rachel were waiting for their art to be shipped to them, making its slow transit from North Texas, she told me about a beautiful painting on the wall behind Craig's office desk in St. Paul. She said that she always wanted to commission artwork, but knew no artists with whom she felt could collaborate on a creative project. She was delighted that David found me, since it was Craig who had contacts in the world of art and design.

As a musician, Craig never expected to be immersed in the world of visual art. But he was suddenly assigned the role of the Interim Chair of the Department of Art and Design. What he assumed would be a brief stint in the world of art ended up lasting two years!

Craig's colleague in the Art Department remembered his passion for coffee, while continually declaring that he would someday shift to tea. As a coffee enthusiast myself I doubt that day would ever have come, even if he lived longer!

He also loved fountain pens. Aren't we humans the strangest mix of interests and passions?

He maintained regular hours at the Department of Art and Design while he was still Dean of the College of Arts and Humanities. One colleague, who had regular interactions with him during those years, offered an amusing perspective on this musician turned art overseer of their College. No one disputed his visionary gifts and his leadership ability that were amply expressed in the field of music. But it was this unplanned immersion in visual art that revealed both his gravitas and quirky sense of humor.

He would frequently, jokingly express his concern about identifying art.

"Is that ART?" was a regular quip of his.

This was asked of the many mundane objects that he encountered, acknowledging their bizarre potential to perhaps be *"objets d'art!"* His response would be tempered by the answer supplied by others to that essential question. Judging from the many absurd things that are gravely categorized by *"art experts"* as contemporary art, his was not a crazy question!

He once learned that a putty installation, which looked like an unclean mess to be dealt with, was actually a student's artwork!

When exposed to ideas and work that defied his

understanding of what should aesthetically qualify as art, he proceeded cautiously, but with the inherent honesty that was an integral part of his nature.

Craig, you are no longer with us on earth, having graduated to heaven, yet as the artist of this work, commissioned by David for your beloved Rachel, the question you often asked intrigues me.

"Would my painting qualify?

Is it ART?"

Unfortunately, I'll have to wait for my answer. I have yet a few brief days left yet on this earth, before I meet him in eternity.

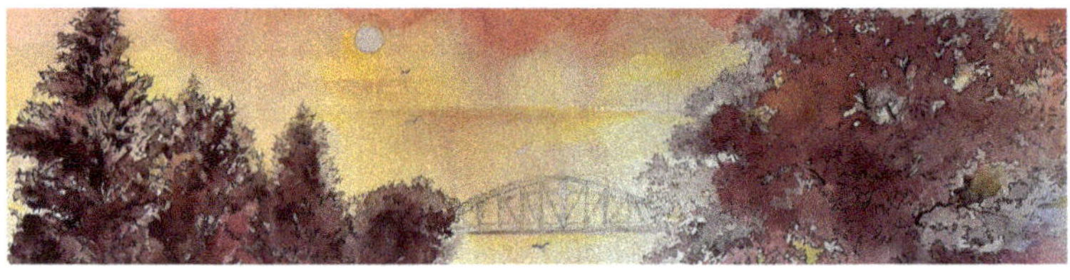

27

I Am Comforted

DAVID: SATURDAY, JULY 30, 2022

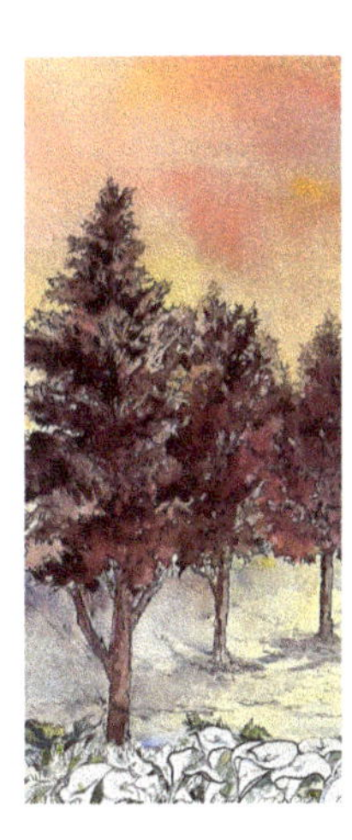

Today I contemplate God's gift to me. What love, what compassion and mercy— that a Holy God would comfort a broken sinner like me!

I am so humbled, my mind is stretched and my heart encouraged. Imagine Christ's own joy is increased as He pours out His grace onto me!

> *"Looking unto Jesus*
> *the author and finisher of our faith;*
> *who for the joy*
> *that was set before him*
> *endured the cross,*
> *despising the shame,*
> *and is set down at the right hand*
> *of the throne of God."*
> Hebrews 12:2 KJV

At 7 a.m. Kevin came over for coffee. We had a great conversation about what real accountability looks like in a true friend. You can't have a deep friendship with everyone, so what should define it?

At its core, true friendship ought to continually point each other to Christ and encourage growth in godliness. We should also constantly be gaining a heightened awareness of those hurting around us. My joy should be increased as I extend grace to my friends and family.

True friendship and accountability is so much more than pursuing purity of mind. It's caring deeply enough so that you're sharing all aspects of life—work, children, wife, extended family... I should be treasuring relationships so much that I would continually ask for prayer and help.

Just like I pursue knowledge and seek experienced people in my career, I should be seeking experienced advice and prayer for the nuances in life that I encounter in the many personal relationships that I treasure!

Real relationships matter—showing great love—it's about my actions and reactions. It's about being present and listening.

What a great conversation Kevin and I had! I look forward to coffee with him again, and would like to pull Kent in as well, so we can start building true deep friendships. I so need this!

I laid down for a brief nap before the chaos of the day began. I've invited a small crowd for dinner tonight. I'm smoking ribs and making coleslaw and vegetables! As the day unfolded, I received several pictures from my family in Pensacola. I always enjoy seeing the memories they are making!

Dinner was ok. The ribs were an epic fail on moistness. They were dried out and chewy, but they tasted great! I hosted Flynn Jones from my work, along with the Marleys and a neighborhood kid that is always hanging out at their place. The night finished with Luke and Clara stopping by to eat leftovers.

What a full day!

O God, my heart is so full of thankfulness for the peace and comfort you continue to provide.

SUNDAY, JULY 31, 2022

This morning I review the pictures taken the week before Jenny's death. Oh, how I treasure those days—the ice cream date—priceless—so also the dinner by the pool! Putting lotion on her feet the morning of... I chuckle at how she couldn't stand Hazel licking the lotion off her feet, but it was quite ok for Maisie to do so!

At church, I sat with Jenny's parents and listened as Pastor taught through Proverbs. We looked at work and wealth. On the subject of work, we examined the diligence of the ant contrasted with a lazy person. On wealth we looked at how it is a gift from God to be used for Him.

After church, I had a great meeting with Pat. At the funeral home, he pulled me close before he left and gave me a beautiful charge, reminding me of the opportunity that God has now given me to use my time and words wisely.

On Saturday, when Kevin and I discussed friendships that glorified God, we talked out loud about who we knew that honored God well. Who did we know who was not pushy, or in your face? I came up with Pastor and Kevin reminded me of Pat. I immediately texted him asking for a time on Sunday to meet.

I spent two and a half hours with Pat on Sunday afternoon as he invested in me. He reflected on how God has been transforming him through the years.

He said that there are two kinds of men in church—those dressed up, and others who are dressed up and messed up! That's me! Dressed up and messed up—a sinner in need of a great Savior!

I reflected on my conversations with men in church through the years. Those conversations match what Pat attested to. He said that we engage in fake conversations leading to emptiness. Instead, we could tear down walls that have taken years to build and find out what it's like to be an authentic man of Jesus.

As I leaned into his experience, learning about being more intentional in relationships at church, I asked, *"How? How are you doing this?"*

"Become less of you. Become vulnerable, transparent and compassionate—always loving, and never judging. Be intentional, and each time you do this it allows you to become more authentic," he answered.

So basically, be more like my humble and lowly Jesus!

> *"He must increase,*
> *but I must decrease."*
> John 3:30 KJV

This resonates with all I have been learning these past weeks.

Dinner tonight was with the girls and their husbands. It was a great time together with some tasty bites. I asked for everyone's partnership over dinner.

"As I reflected on God's work of grace in my life—the strength, joy, and comfort that I have to overflowing, I need you to love me enough to tell me when you see something choking my walk with Christ. Speak up when you see me act, or react, to life in a way that is stealing my joy in Christ!"

We then discussed what true friendship looks like. I am so very great-full to God for my family. What an encouragement they are to me!

As I continue to memorize Psalm 34, my heart leaps for joy as I realize that what David wrote is what I am literally experiencing! The tittle of the psalm is *"The Lord, a Provider and the One Who Rescues Me."*

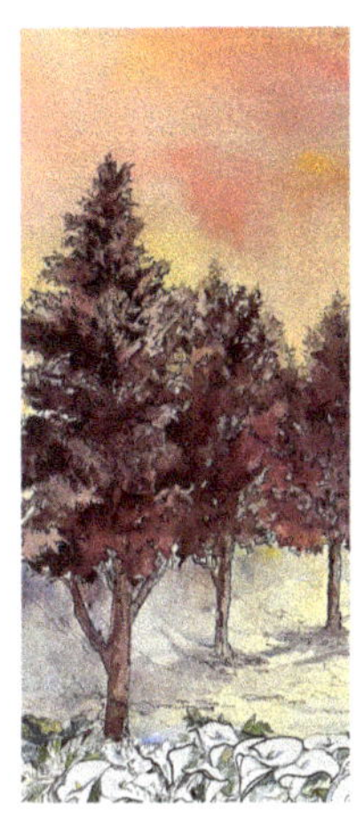

My great God has rescued me! I am wholly and utterly dependent on Him. This dependence on Him has clearly shown me that I had previously replaced Him with self-sufficiency and control. May He increase my dependence on Him so that I release all control to Him.

How wonderful that God would reach down and pull me close to Him! My very desires have been changed!

At work I often say I am an artist trying to figure this IT (Information Technology) thing out. Now I am internalizing that I am a believer trying to learn all about my wonderful Savior and Redeemer!

Oh God, open my eyes to see my sin and allow me to grow in my understanding of you so that I might more quickly bring my brokenness to you.

Make me new so that my desire is to serve and honor you in all I do. Make me more like you so that I can serve others well.

28

Is His Grace Sufficient?

Oh, how thankful I am that Christ gave me new life—that He *would* change me, that He *is* changing me!

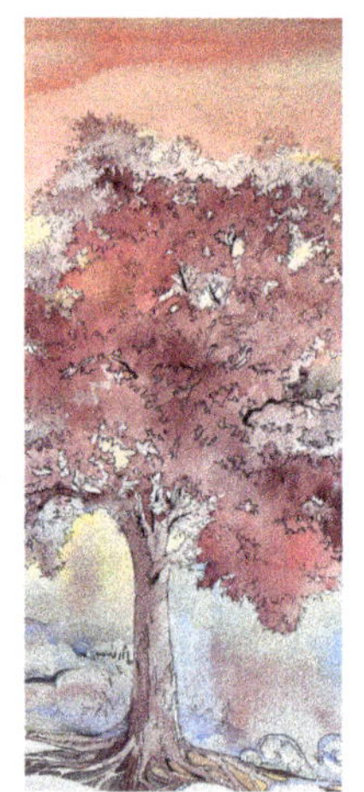

He didn't turn away from me in my darkest hour of need. Instead, He pulled me close and held me fast. He gave me strength and comfort like I have never had before.

Instead of lamenting that things were different, I trust that God is for me. I pray for help to exchange my feelings for the truth.

Justification is tied to what Christ did in the past.

Intercession is what He's doing in the present. An intercessor doesn't simply stand between the two parties as an advocate, but steps over and joins one party as He approaches the other!

As my mind takes this all in afresh, my heart is encouraged and comforted. That God would send His perfect son, Jesus, to this earth to die a death He didn't deserve, which pays for my sins—so that all who call on Him might be justified. That is so hard for me to wrap my mind around! What does that mean really?

To be justified is to be declared "righteous." But how can I, a sinner, be declared "righteous?"

As I look up the word "righteous" I am reminded that to be declared "righteous" means to be free from guilt or sin. So justification is an act of God, whereby He pronounces me, a sinner, to be "righteous," because of my faith in Christ!

I am so very thankful for my salvation and to know that Jesus is now continually interceding, advocating, and in communication with God on my behalf! When I don't know what to pray and I just cry out helplessly, He does, and is, praying for me!

I wrapped up my journaling just in time to head to work a little early this morning. I have a breakfast scheduled with Dustin. I have great memories of going to the Saint Francis home and donating time building Christmas boxes for the homeless with Jenny. This is a charity that is near and dear to Dustin's heart.

As I head to breakfast, I beg God to give me the opportunity to share with him what God is doing in my life.

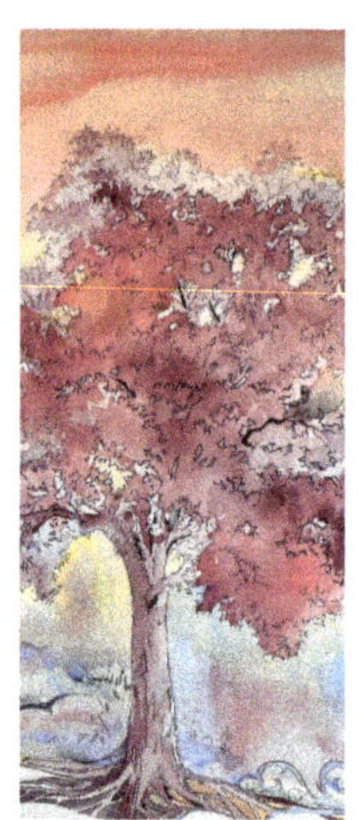

Over breakfast, I express the joy that I have on one hand, and the grief that I have on the other. But the fact is that I've got joy to overflowing! I am in awe of the strength that God has been to me and the comfort that He provides daily.

Dustin expressed that he could not fathom how that was so. He's had so much grief in his life. A year ago his wife's cousin had a daughter, who was just twenty five years old when she tragically died in a boating accident. His wife's cousin was very angry with God, and a year after her death, she is still angry! Life is quite different for her.

As he contrasted the way his wife's cousin was handling death and how I was handling it, he asked, *"David, as you look at your life is there a certain point that you saw God being different—more real, or closer do you?*

"Yes!" I exclaim.

I see two distinct periods of time that God has been real

to me. Once when I was a child, I cried out to God. Yet, I saw myself going through the years minimally transformed.

But then I see the days immediately after Jenny's death crying out to God differently. I begged God to change, comfort and strengthen me.

He became very real to me, when I became wholly dependent on him.

Dustin and I had a very sweet time together rejoicing in what He is doing in my life. I shared words of comfort and strength for him to share with his wife, as she seeks to minister to her cousin in her greatest time of need.

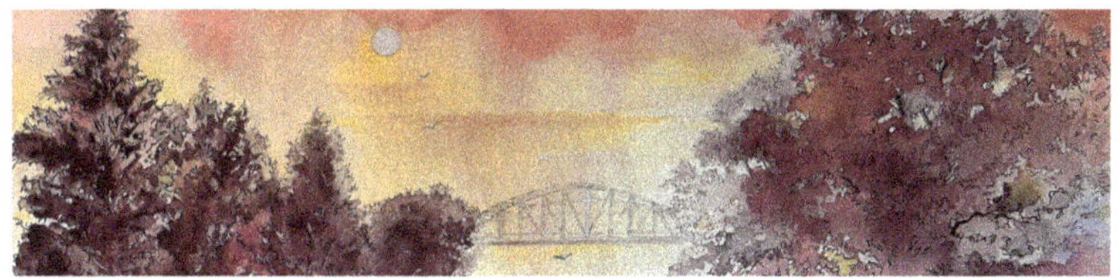

29

Crooked Paths Leading
to Life

DAVID: FRIDAY, AUGUST 5, 2022

As I look at my life, I see two clear markers in time. The first was when I came to Christ, and the other was when I decided to devote my life to Him in its entirety, determined to become like Him!

> *"As the deer pants for the water brooks,*
> *So my soul pants for You, God."*
> Psalm 42:1 NKJV

Jenny had long been the spiritual leader in my home, and I was content to allow God to transform me in a very limited way.

For the past twenty five years of my marriage, there were continual cycles of dis-engagement.

I treated my spiritual growth and com-mitment to Christ like a New Year's resolu-tion—this year I am going to read my Bible, pray, do my devotions, be a better husband, a better father...

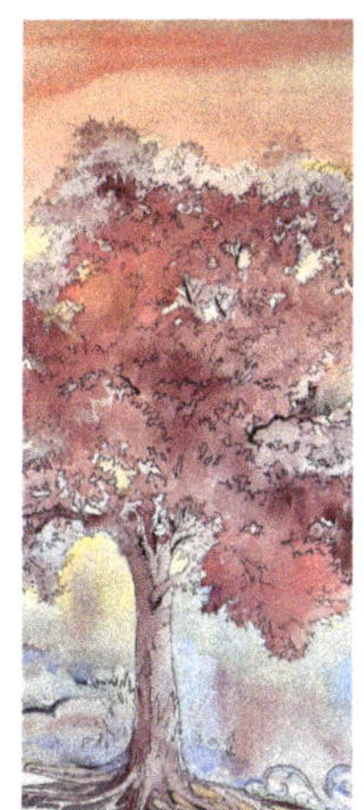

And for twenty five years I continually failed!

Two years ago, I decided once again that I was going to take my spiritual growth more seriously. But this time, I was going to add a layer, I was going to get some accountability in my devotions.

Jenny told me that I needed Proverbs 3:5-7

"Trust in the LORD with all your heart,
And lean not on your own understanding;

> *In all your ways acknowledge Him,*
> *And He shall direct your paths.*
> *Do not be wise in your own eyes;*
> *Fear the LORD and depart from evil."*
> Proverbs 3:5-7 NKJV

But I still didn't need Him. God was more like a genie that I took out when I hit a wall.

After Thanksgiving, I found myself in hospital, because I allowed myself to think about what would life be like without Jenny. By 11 a.m. I was in the Emergency Room.

Now she is gone and I can't even breathe without His help. So I sat for forty-eight hours with no sleep, filling my mind with His word in song.

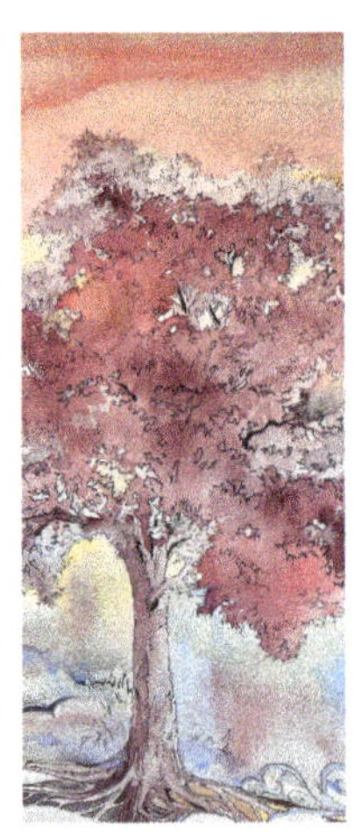

The days immediately following her death I clearly see as the second marker in time. I am now wholly committed to serving Him and His will. How can I not? I have such peace, comfort and strength—I should be in the hospital!

As I cry out to God continually, He starts showing me my sin. ALL of it—calling me to repentance. Repentance—true repentance for deep-seated entitlement and pride. I spend time thinking and pondering how I have sinned against my great God. I sat in those thoughts.

That was true grief.

I then sought accountability partners, true friends. I told them that this is where I am, this is how I am struggling. Will you be on my accountability team and check in on me to ask me how I am doing in these areas?

I continually beg God for transformational grace—show me more—change me, make me new and soften my heart. I do this hour by hour, and sometimes minute by minute!

"So David," you might ask, *"where do we see this in the Word, why are you so amped up about begging and pleading...?"*

It's what God calls us to. The apostle Paul modeled this well for us. I beseech you, brethren ... I implore... beg, plead...

"I beseech you therefore, brethren, by the mercies of God,
that ye present your bodies a living sacrifice, holy,
acceptable unto God,
which is your reasonable service."
Romans" 12:1 KJV

Paul is pleading ... do this! There are no qualifiers saying that this is only for pastors. This is us all, sinners, in need of a great God and His transformational grace! He even says ... *"this is your reasonable service .. "*

We see this again in Titus.

> *"For the grace of God that brings salvation*
> *has appeared to all men,*
> *teaching us that, denying ungodliness*
> *and worldly lusts,*
> *we should live soberly, righteously,*
> *and godly in the present age,*
> *looking for the blessed hope*
> *and glorious appearing of our great God*
> *and Savior Jesus Christ,*
> *who gave Himself for us,*
> *that He might redeem us*
> *from every lawless deed*
> *and purify for Himself*
> *His own special people,*
> *zealous for good works."*
> Titus 2:11-14 NKJV

This is the daily discipline we are called to. We can't do this alone. It requires a life wholly given to His service. I can't tell you how many times I have tried over the last many years!

The emotions evoked from the death of my Jenny have a very short shelf life, but the emotions and real heart change of God's transformation is eternal!

I can't even get out of bed without Him.

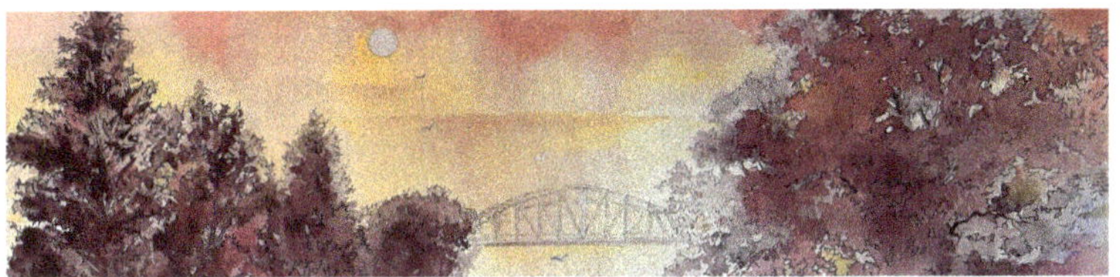

30

Jenny's Closet

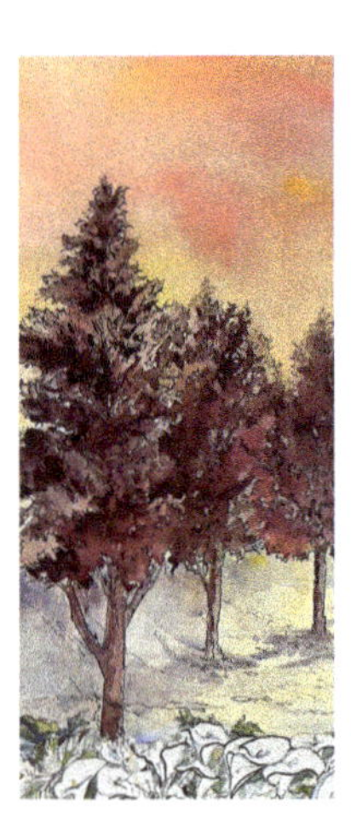

This evening the girls are coming over and we are emptying Jenny's closet and vanity. Liz arrived first. We talk about grief and how good God has been to me to give me so many resources. Each morning has been a sweet time of mourning, meditation and reflection.

To think God would give me the strength, at day 48, to be going though Jenny's clothes and emptying out her dresser!

The girls and I went through each item of clothing. What memories!

"Boy, I loved that blouse—it looked so great on her" to
"I don't know what she saw in that .. I never cared for that on her!"

God, I stand in awe of you! You have taught me to pursue you with my whole heart. Everything else flows out of that. Instead of all my responsibilities being so daunting, things that overwhelm me, they have become a source of great joy as you empower me to do your will—making my burden light! My job is pursue you, know you, delight in you, and follow you in obedience. And you transform!

Time is the most valuable resource we have. I am so very thankful for the time God gave me with Jenny. I wish I had better used my time and had spent more time with her. And yet, time with her is what I am most thankful for.

I must have a proper understanding of future glory. This life is so momentary. I try to wrap my mind around how short my life is in relationship to eternity! Even if my life is filled with one hardship after the next, I will still have eternity with Christ. This perspective then allows me to not lose heart. It keeps my eyes up and fixed on Him.

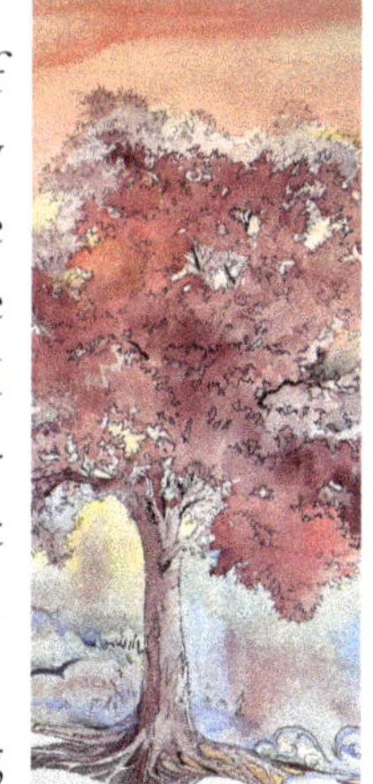

We must be proactive about cultivating godly emotions. Our life is like a garden, one we must tend to by removing those weeds that attempt to choke out our joy.

> " I went by the field of the lazy man,
> And by the vineyard of the man devoid of
> understanding;
> And there it was,
> all overgrown with thorns;
> Its surface was covered with nettles;
> Its stone wall was broken down.
> When I saw it, I considered it well;
> I looked on it and received instruction:"
> Proverbs 24:30 -32

Pastor encouraged us to think soberly about how we are tending to the garden of our mind. It requires an honest self evaluation with God's word.

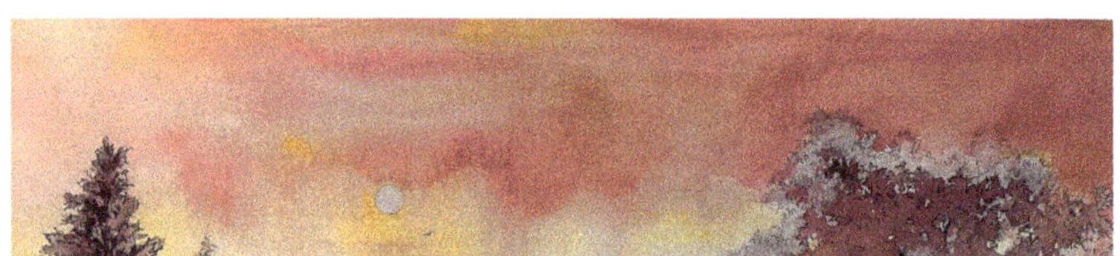

31

Twin Daughters

I love the recent photo of mom at my wedding. We are standing outside the barn, before the wedding, with the photographer. It's before I have seen anyone.

Mom was the first to see me!

The photographer then set us up for our first photo together. I so love this photo as it reminds me of Mom's laughter. It is a genuinely candid photo! The photographer had just told us to make a funny face at 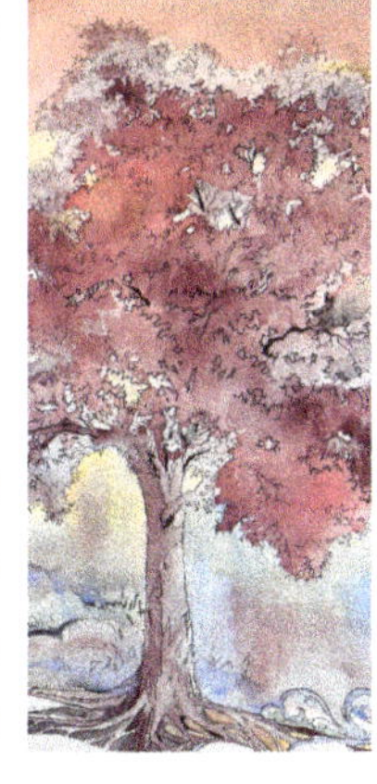 each other, which made us laugh! We told him that we didn't want to make a funny face. Oddly enough that resulted in a terrific photo filled with laughter!

It now hangs above my coffee bar.

CLARA

I love the photo from our wedding. Mom is standing waiting for Luke and me to exit the church and head out to the limo. Soon we would be off to our honeymoon. Dad is standing behind her with his hands on her shoulders.

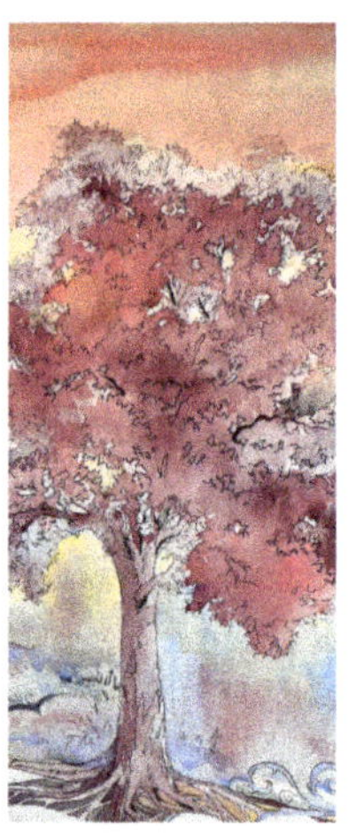

The look on her face evokes such fond memories of her in my mind. She was so involved in that day and was so happy to see Luke and me off.

I know that day was tough for her, as she told me, and others, that it would be. Yet she was excited to see us happy to start our lives together. That photo just reminds me of the many conversations we had about how excited we were for this day.

She and I were so close, sharing such fun memories with each other. I am reminded of the joy she had for everyone and everything that she loved. She shared in our joy SO MUCH.

LIZ

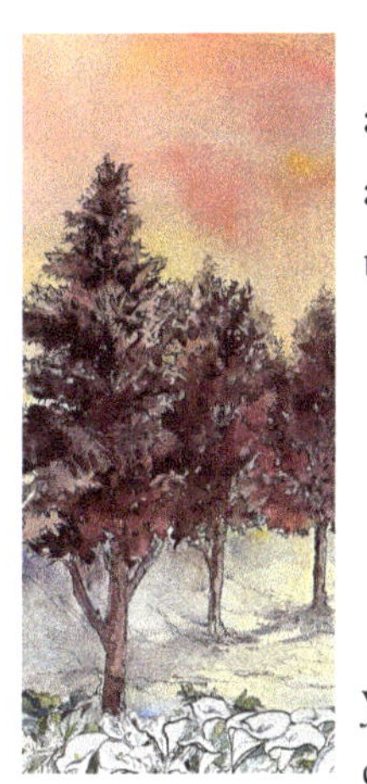

I am so thankful to God that we were able to have my wedding before Mom's death and that I have this special memory so close to her death.

CLARA

I am thankful that God gave me three years of being married to Luke before she died. Mom and I were very close. I feel if this had happened three years earlier (if I had been in Liz's shoes) this would have been way harder for me.

Don't get me wrong, it's still really difficult for me. I treasure Mom, her opinions, and all that she meant to me. But I am so thankful that God gave me Luke, because I really have needed him. I've seen that our relationship has been, and will continue to be, solidified because of this.

LIZ

Countless times before Mom's passing, I remember standing in church and singing songs, without ever thinking about the words. Now, I find myself reflecting on the words in the songs, sometimes even coming to the point of tears!

Probably just two short weeks after Mom had passed away, we sang *"Christ, Our Hope in Life and Death"* at Bentwood. I could not even get through the first few words! This song holds so much truth in it. It also is such a special song to me, because it was the last one I got to sing with Mom!

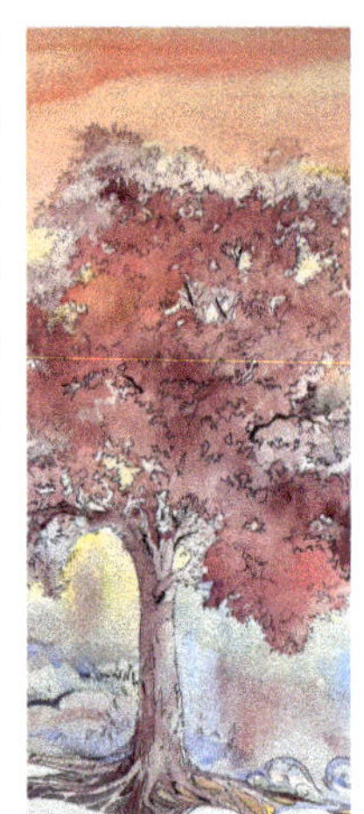

CLARA

I am really encouraged by the words of the hymn, *Standing on the Promises*, because it reminds me of our present circumstances.

"Standing on the promises that cannot fail,
When the howling storms of doubt and fear assail,
By the living Word of God I shall prevail,
Standing on the promises of God."

We need to simply rest in the promises of God in our trials. That is exactly what I have done since Mom's death. The only way I have been able to somehow make it through is by standing on His very precious promises.

I know I have the future hope of seeing Mom again. I also know I will be strengthened by Him every step of the way, as I have already been.

It has been really, really tough! I have moments when I am just really sad. I don't fight it but just sit in that. As I remind myself of His promises, He renews, refreshes and encourages me. His promises to help me do the impossible.

I no longer feel defeated.

32

Make Three Wishes

I thank God for a bundle of resources that Rachel gave me.

These are resources that she found helpful, carefully categorized, born out of a heart that sought after God.

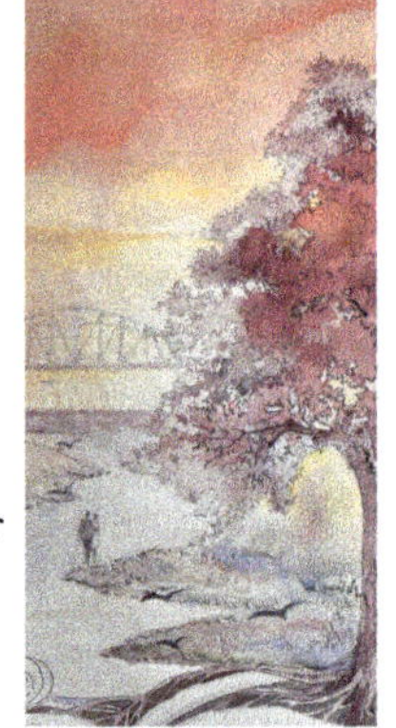

She also, in wisdom, sat in the house of mourning for two years.

There, she, like me, found great comfort, strength and transformation through Christ.

DAVID: TUESDAY, AUGUST 23, 2022

I was asked an odd question today.

" If you had a genie and could make three wishes, what would they be?" "Take your time," I was told.

"You may need to think on this and come back next week to answer."

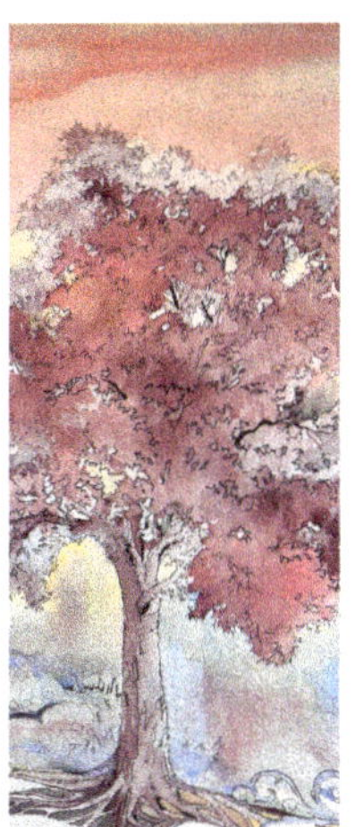

I don't need time! I only have one wish, not three.

I wish to know my Great God and Savior completely! I know so little about Him and am desperate to learn more.

"Hmmm," he said, *"Well, what if, with the two remaining wishes, you could look into the future and know that anything you hoped for would come true.*

What is your vision for two to three years in the future?"

I quickly answered that I don't really have any desire to try to figure out the future.

God gives me grace for today and does not promise me tomorrow. So I would want to serve Him today with all my heart.

33

Grandpa's Letter to Laura

DAVID

Hello, Ms. Laura.

Welcome to this beautiful world that our great God created for you to enjoy!

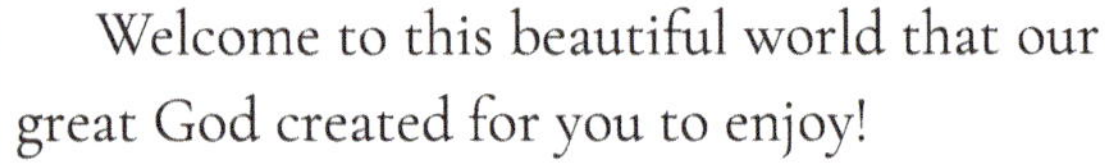

Grandma Jenny and I have been waiting for you with much anticipation. As I sit here this morning, looking into the kitchen, I can still remember the day your Mom and Dad shared the news of your pending arrival.

As all good parents, they found a very creative way to announce you. We were asked to help them

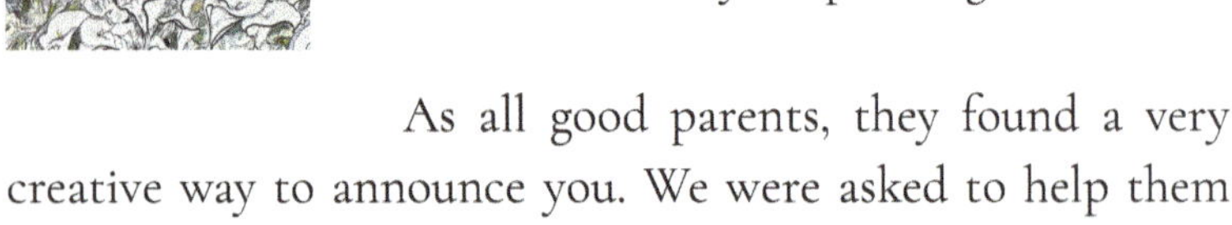

settle a dispute over which shoes to buy. They had slipped in a pair of baby shoes among our choices!

At first we skipped right past them. Then we were prompted to go back quickly!

Baby shoes? What?

"Oh, my GOODNESS!" your grandmother shrieked, *"Clara, you're PREGNANT? REALLY?"*

She ran around the kitchen island and gave you your very first hug! She had been praying for this very day to arrive for over a year now, and it was finally here! We both couldn't believe it.

God had a very special plan for your grandmother. The months that followed was a journey of God's difficult, but good, providence. It was filled with much love and grace as she prepared for your arrival.

She would want you to know of her love for her great God. She knew that without His love she was incapable of loving others as He did. Jesus came into our world that we might have LIGHT and LIFE, through His death on the cross in payment for our sins. He gives us grace upon grace.

Your grandmother was a recipient of that grace. She enjoyed His love, compassion, and the gift of eternal life! She was transformed daily as she sought to live a life pleasing to

Him. That same great grace flowed outward to others, allowing her to love as Christ loved.

Grandma adored your mother, Clara! She invested so very selflessly in her as she grew up, modeling a Christlike love. His Spirit then placed a deep desire in her also to please Him at an early age! Your mother will be modeling this same selfless love to you as you also grow up!

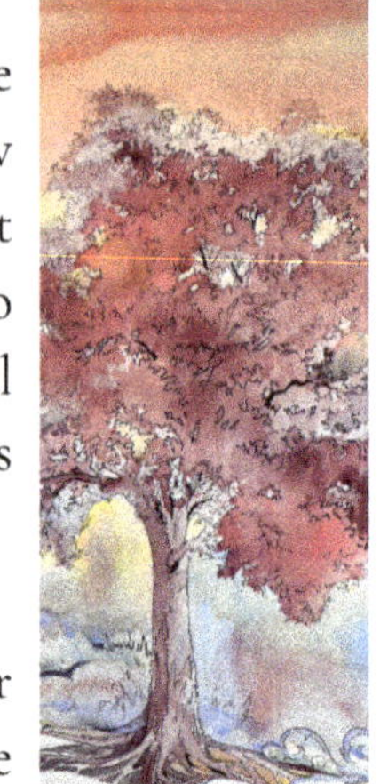

Each time you receive love from your dear mother, remember that it is from the inheritance she received from our gracious God. That same God, who formed, loved, and transformed your grandmother is the One who is transforming your mother.

Grandma Jenny is not here in this world to hold you or to walk beside you. However, your Creator, the God of the universe, has made some very precious promises that will sustain your parents. We pray that those same promises will one day sustain you as well.

There will be many difficult days ahead for you and your parents, as you grow and experience firsthand the effects of sin in our world. My prayer is that you learn about your Creator and His plan and purpose for you.

Grief and pain are all part of the curse of sin on this

world. When you grow up and experience it, I pray that you will learn that your Creator will redeem its harmful effects in your life.

> "The LORD is near to those
> who have a broken heart,
> And saves such as have a contrite spirit."
> Psalm 34:18 NKJV
>
> "Come unto me, all ye that labour
> and are heavy laden,
> and I will give you rest.
> Take my yoke upon you, and learn of me;
> for I am meek and lowly in heart:
> and ye shall find rest unto your souls.
> For my yoke is easy, and my burden is light."
> Matthew 11:28-30 KJV
>
> "Suffer little children to come unto me,
> and forbid them not:
> for of such is the kingdom of God.
> Verily I say unto you,
> Whosoever shall not receive
> the kingdom of God as a little child
> shall in no wise enter therein."
> Luke 18: 16-17 KJV

Laura, we pray that God, who made you and loves you, will open your eyes at a young age to see Him and be transformed. Then may you also receive the great inheritance that your Creator placed within your grandmother.

She looks down upon you from heaven. She is now one among the great cloud of witnesses!

Know your Creator. Love Him! Serve Him, and honor your parents.

Much love,
Grandpa David

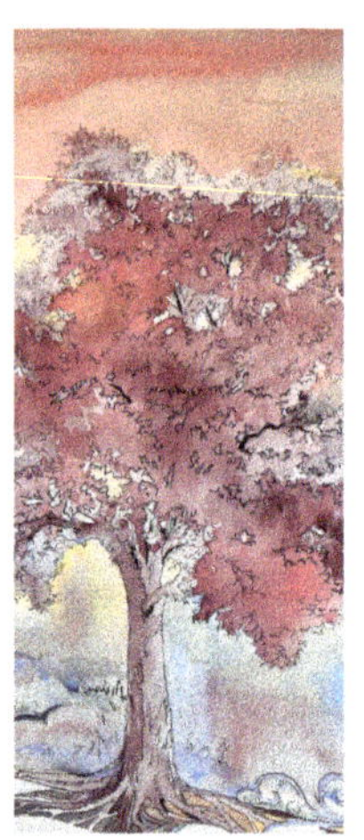

34

I, David, Take You Jenny

DAVID: TUESDAY, AUG 23, 2022

"I Love you Forever and Ever" is how she started her card to me just 49 days before we had the most beautiful wedding!

Jenny went on to say in that same card, *"The words of this card can only begin to describe how I feel about you. I love you so much that neither words nor gifts could display how much! I cannot wait for 49 days from now, when you will most definitely make me the happiest woman alive. I love you and I never, ever, ever want that thought to leave your mind."*

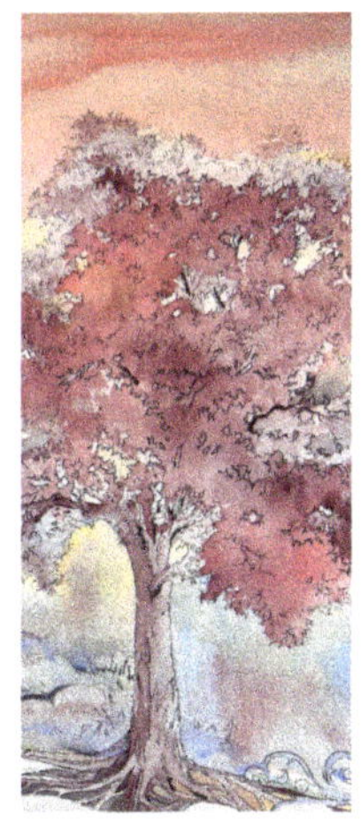

When we got engaged in Pensacola, I sang *"Yours Forever"* to her, and then sang that same song on our wedding day.

"When the sun is shining bright, I'll be yours forever
When you face the darkest night, we will face it together..."

On our wedding day I vowed ...

I, David, take you Jenny, to be my lawfully wedded wife, to have and to hold from this day forward, for better or for worse, for richer, for poorer, in sickness and in health, to love and to cherish; from this day forward until death do us part...

I love you forever and ever.

I love you and I never, ever, ever want that thought to leave your mind.

Until death, we will never part.

Until death do us part.

Death has parted us now!

As I look back at these past 25 years, I am so great-full to God for the temporary gift He gave me in Jenny. I am most great-full to God for her diligence in seeking Him about how to raise our children. We were blessed with beautiful twin girls. Jenny pointed their hearts to Christ and faithfully worked with them to steer them away from the fear of man. She instilled in them a deep desire to love God!

I will forever be great-full for the memories I have of her and for the time we had together. *"Forever"* for our marriage was 25 years.

But *"forever"* in heaven, with my Great God and Jenny, will be an eternity!

I never, ever, ever want thoughts of Jenny to fade, but I know they will as time goes on.

The one thought I pray that never fades is that of my dear Savior, who died for me and has sustained me through her death. He is the One, who has restored the joy of my salvation! He has placed my feet on a rock that I may stand firmly to tell others about Jenny's great God— and now MY GREAT GOD!!

Oh God, my words are so feeble and inadequate to describe the love you have shown me!

As I approached this very day of my wedding anniversary, I was quite fearful and overwhelmed with sadness and heaviness of heart.

Then you sent Alan to encourage me. Each day you comforted and reminded me that your grace is sufficient for the day I am in. You instructed me to take no thought for tomorrow, stay in today.

One step at a time. Your peace and comfort, of a sort that only you can provide, has been building in me each day. I find myself more fully resting in you, my Great God!

I praise you now that this day is here and I find myself no longer restless in my spirit. In my fear, I was anticipating a tidal wave of sorrow and you have given me a tidal wave of peace that passes all human understanding!

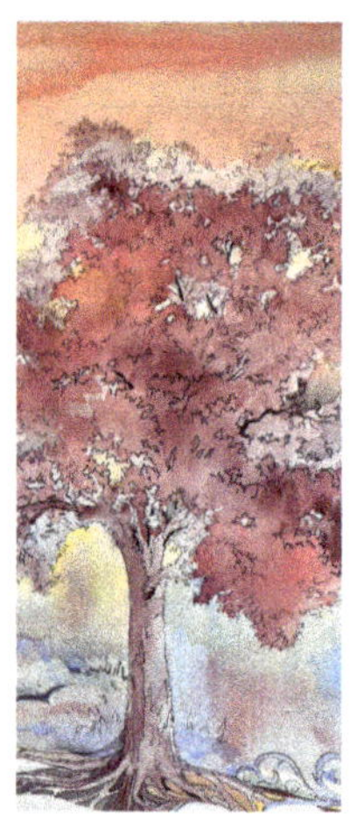

Thank you God for loving me, for sustaining and drawing me close to you, so that I might become more like you. May I best honor Jenny's memory by serving, and loving you, with my whole heart. I love you, God!

I finish up my journal entry and get dressed, heading out to the kitchen to make breakfast. As I do, I marvel that I have complete comfort and peace!

Oh, I so miss Jenny dearly, but my grief has changed from deep sorrow to a fixed expectation that I will see her again.

I turn my focus on glorifying my great God, instead.

35

Memorial on Mackinac Island

I sit in my living room in such deep and abiding peace, basking in the tidal wave of His comfort. It was a sweet time spent reflecting on what today might bring, as we head to Mackinac Island.

As I pick up Kent and Iris, I praise God. My grief is culminating in a great joy and a peace that passes all human understanding!

Do I miss Jenny? Oh my, yes!

It's just no longer this deep, painful sorrow.

Conversation is so sweet as we fly, wait at layover and finally land in Michigan. On the short ride to Mackinac island by the ferry, I hear the story from Iris about how Jenny picked Mackinac Island for our 25th anniversary.

It was at the lake this year that she and Iris were brainstorming about where to go. Iris recommended Mackinac Island, because she felt it best matched Jenny's love for quaint little towns with cute old stores. Then there was priceless scenery and a hotel built in the late 1800s with its rich history!

We reached the hotel by a horse-drawn carriage. No vehicles are allowed on the island, just bikes and horses. What a beautiful sight, although all that horse poop smell is quite offensive!

Once checked into my room, my bag arrived immediately. I changed into running clothes to get a run in before dinner. What a run it was! I ran completely around the island—8.2 miles. It is definitely the best run I've had all year. There's not a bad view from anywhere on the island. I'm so looking forward to making memories together this weekend.

Dinner was quite an affair! In the main dining room, you're only allowed entrance if you are wearing a suit, coat and tie! As we walk to our table, I see smiling, engaged faces and marvel at this beautiful sight. Dinner with Kent and Iris was truly delightful as I told them what God is doing in my heart, rejoicing in His grace and goodness to me!

Oh God, friends and friendship—what a sweet and precious gift true friendship is—this God honoring relationship that points me to Christ! May you knit our hearts closer together this weekend, pointing to the comfort and strength that only You can provide. May we remind each other of your truth and precious promises.

Give us much wisdom on how to best minister to family this week, as we seek to create memories and enjoy each other's company.

THURSDAY, AUGUST 25, 2022

What a terrific, rainy day of memory making we had, lived under the umbrella!

We walked downtown to the shops, stopping at each fudge shop to buy a small wedge. We were conducting a taste test, determined to discover who made the best fudge on the island. It is definitely a job Jenny would have loved—she so loved chocolate!

We stepped into many of the stores, remarking throughout the day how much she would have enjoyed this place. Eventually we stopped for lunch at the storied Pink Pony, enjoyed some very tasty bites, then wandered around to more shops, before getting in a carriage for a tour of the island, entertained by a chatty tour guide!

We got back to the hotel by 5 p.m, in time to rest, before dinner at 6:30 p.m.

We sat out on the front porch waiting for everyone to come down before standing in line to enter the grand dining room for dinner. The formal affair that is dinner added a great spark to the air as everyone was all dressed up. The ladies looked terrific, while us, guys, were being choked by our ties!

Dinner was a five course meal, a two and a half hour event, including dessert—terrific conversation, memories shared and new ones made!

After dinner, we retired to the parlor area to study Psalm 40 for a bit, before moving to my room for a couple hands of Shanghai—Jenny's favorite game!

Thank you, God!

FRIDAY, AUGUST 26, 2022

The morning started with a 5 mile run and breakfast with the family at 8:30 a.m. The girls and their husbands then headed out to play a round of golf. The pictures we received back from them throughout the day were amazing—spectacular views of the island and lake, while on the course!

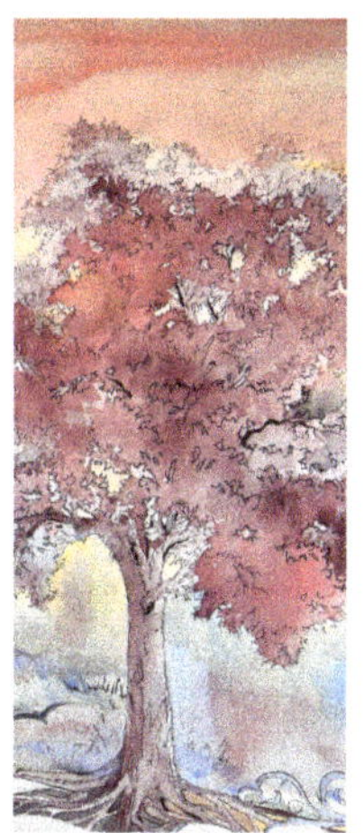

While they golfed, Iris, Kent and I, started our morning on the porch reading. I then decided to start a simple marriage survey for select guests. We saw that we were the young people at the Grand Hotel, since the average age of most that stayed here was 70!

"Excuse me, Ma'am, would you like to participate in my marriage survey, please? It's a one question survey."

"How long have you been married?," I ask.

She quickly responds, with a great smile *"Fifty three!"*

Her husband quips with a grin *" Fifty two!"*

"Oh, so you're not claiming the first year of marriage then?"

I learn they are here, like many, celebrating their wedding anniversary. Another couple made themselves willing survey participants, as they struggled to get a good picture with a digital camera from the 90's!

I had to help. So I slipped over and took their picture with my phone. As they moved to another spot on the porch for more pictures, I learned this is their fiftieth anniversary!

I email the pictures to them.

The husband asked what he could do for me since I was so helpful.

I told him with a great big smile, *"Love your dear wife well!"*

36

Rachel's Promise Gift

DAVID: DECEMBER, 2022

Rachel, I am the beneficiary of Craig's leadership, love and devotion to you and Christ.

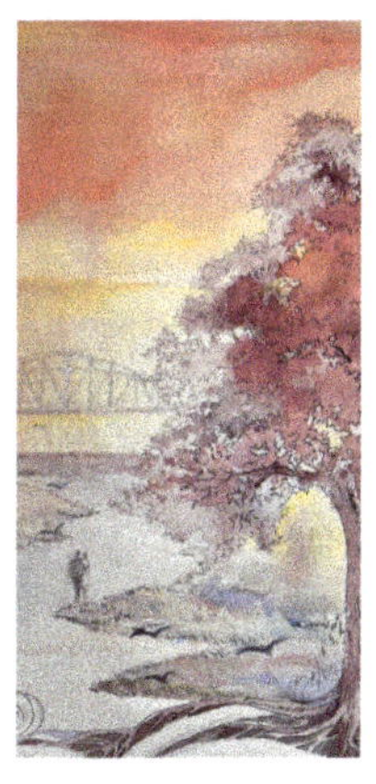

Today, I give you a Promise Ring as we await our engagement in January. I had this Promise Ring made for you to signify the uniqueness of our great God's story, written on our hearts. It is now our story filled with grace and truth—a story of transformation, sanctification and redemption.

When we do the hard work of forgiving and forbearing, our affections will flourish. God will be glorified, when two very different people forge a life of faithfulness, by wholly relying on Christ.

We can't do this, Rachel, but He can, if we will rely on Him.

He will purify and refine us, just like this diamond I give you, was refined as it was formed!

Every time you look at this yellow diamond in the future, I pray it will be a great reminder that we are broken sinners in need of grace. We are going to hurt each other.

Sin hurts. It is dirty, and without forgiveness, forbearance and grace, we will never be formed into the testimony He designed us to be!

Rachel, this is my promise to you. Do you accept my promise?

Rachel: *"YES!!! Absolutely! You are a gift of God's grace to me!"*

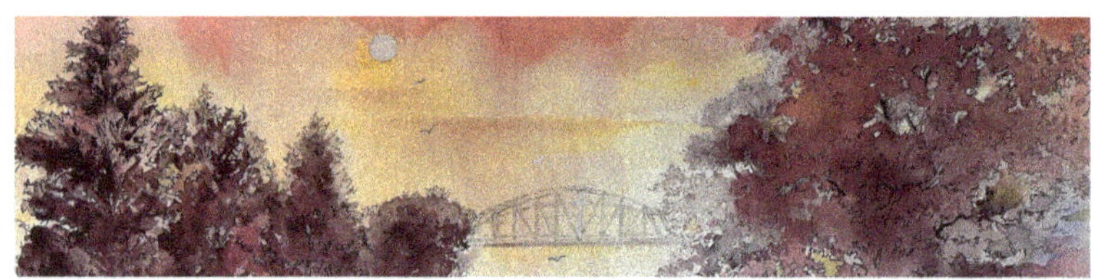

37

The Witnesses

SARA

Filled with thoughts about those who had gone before us in life and those who will follow after us, depicted as birds in the foreground and background, I worked furiously towards my deadline.

My shoulder ached as I made small marks in dark ink over the painted surface. It was a large painting for a watercolor and I was in a race against time.

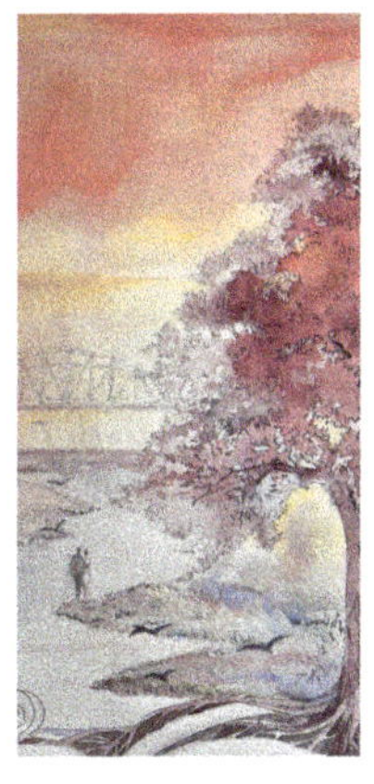

> *"Wherefore seeing we also*
> *are compassed about*
> *with so great a cloud of witnesses,*
> *let us lay aside every weight,*
> *and the sin which doth so easily beset us,*
> *and let us run with patience*
> *the race that is set before us,*
>
> *Looking unto Jesus the author*
> *and finisher of our faith;*
> *who for the joy that was set before him*
> *endured the cross,*
> *despising the shame, and is set down*
> *at the right hand of the throne of God*
>
> *For consider him*
> *that endured such contradiction*
> *of sinners against himself,*
> *lest ye be wearied*
> *and faint in your minds."*
> Hebrews 12:1-3 KJV

Our original agreement was that David would print out a high resolution copy of my grey scale concept sketch for Rachel on the day he proposed to her. He hoped to whet her appetite for the colorful final painting and sweeten the anticipation of the wait. That was the plan until I started working on it.

Then David's excitement at surprising Rachel infected me as well! I love surprises and found myself chuckling with delight as I worked on the painting. But could I somehow get it finished before the evening of his big day? A full color copy would be far better than black and white. It would make his proposal truly special.

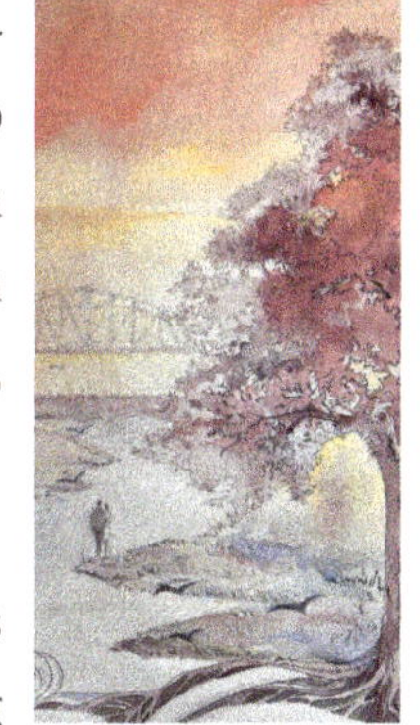

He had sourced a printer, who was waiting for any high resolution image from me to print at short notice. He also had a friend on standby who would bring the print to him on the day. It was now up to me. No pressure, he assured me!

Working out the concept always takes time, as does getting a satisfactory drawing on the paper. In the foreground I placed an open Bible. Then there was a tree close by anchored by spreading roots, drawing nourishment from water, curling in stylized waves, and many other symbolic elements to include in the painting to tell their story.

A good drawing forms the bones of the painting. Watercolors flow quickly—they must, or they will lose freshness and look contrived. Once the paper is stretched and ready for flowing color, everything moves fast. Armed with a blow dryer to tackle stubborn patches of damp paper, I can make the painting move even faster. Controlling the degree of moisture in the paper at all times is an essential skill to develop—a process that is more of an art rather than predictable science! Unexpected accidents can be either frustrating or delightful. That is the charm of watercolor.

Rachel had always loved the colors of sunrise. David shared with me a photo taken on their bridge on the anniversary of Craig's death. Golds and oranges of dawn saturated the photo. Those colors were etched in her very being as meaningful, so all other palette choices had to play softer notes that harmonized with their blazing warmth.

When I finished with the watercolor, I decided to define in ink some shapes that seemed a little too indistinct for my liking. It was drawing those shapes in ink that added hours I had not planned. Hundreds of little ink lines and shapes had to be worked onto the surface of the paper, until it felt complete.

"How late is too late?" I texted David at 10:30 a.m. on the morning of the big day. He told me that I could work until 2 p.m.

In the end, it was almost 3 p.m. (with his permission) when I finally set my pen down and felt the painting was complete! I then hurriedly took a digital image of the art and sent it to the printer, hoping that his friend would still be able to get it to David on time.

My prayers for those who have blessed me with the commission flow continually as I work. I seek God's wisdom for the work and for them. My most exciting moments are when I recognize His help, whether reflected in the work itself or in words that I receive from Him for them.

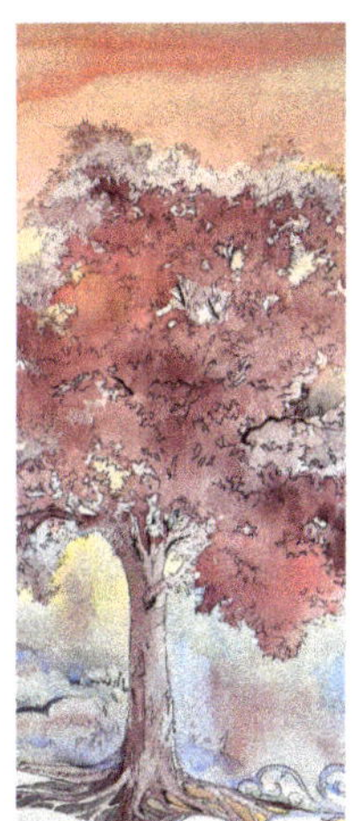

For this painting, I sensed their tears and the long road they had traveled to be able to trust Him, and each other, for the future. So was revealed the first promise that He had for them.

> *They that sow in tears shall reap in joy.*
> *He that goeth forth and weepeth,*
> *bearing precious seed,*
> *shall doubtless come again with rejoicing,*
> *bringing his sheaves with him.*
> Psalm 126:5 -6 KJV

Sowing in tears is a profound act of faith. It is trusting God from a position of vulnerability and weakness. The seeds in their case were seeds of faith in Jesus, despite the sudden harshness of their loss. Their steely determination to trust Him was precious seed sown in tears.

In all sowing there is some measure of trepidation. Will the seed that is sown be lost forever? Should that happen, the sowers would truly be bereft. If one possesses an abundance of seeds to sow, a few lost seeds are no great loss.

Seed that is precious to the sower is seed that is rare. This is seed that the sowers cannot afford to lose, because it is all that the sower has left to sow. It is seed that MUST see increase in fruit. All hope is wrapped up in the act of sowing such precious seed with tears.

Therefore, the promise of rejoicing is because of the disproportional sheaves of harvest that God promises to everyone in covenant partnership with Him. David and Rachel were assured of that.

He had seen their tears, He had walked with them through darkness. Their faith pleased Him and He had a good future planned for them. They were convinced of it, because as they sowed they understood His goodness.

The beauty in their love story lies in the fact that they had a choice individually to walk away from God in the wake of their personal tragedies. Yet they turned to Love Himself, and He re-ignited love, first for Him, and then birthed in them love for one another.

Many, who lose spouses ache with loneliness, and in desperation, step into relationships, neither initiated nor sustained by Jesus. Sadly, these relationships are short lived, deepening the pain and cementing the sense of hopelessness and loss. David and Rachel chose Jesus and He blessed them with each other.

He does all things well.

Paul's timeless words would fit them easily and they became my prayer for them as well.

> *"I thank my God upon*
> *every remembrance of you,*
> *Always in every prayer of mine for you all*
> *making request with joy,*
> *For your fellowship in the gospel*
> *from the first day until now;*
> *Being confident of this very thing,*
> *that he which hath begun*
> *a good work in you*
> *will perform it until*
> *the day of Jesus Christ:"*
> Philippians 1:3-6 KJV

It is indeed *"fellowship in the gospel from the first day until now,"* which made this romance possible. That same passion for the gospel will see this love story through until their time on earth is done.

That's what true love is all about—initiated and sustained by the Author of Love, Jesus.

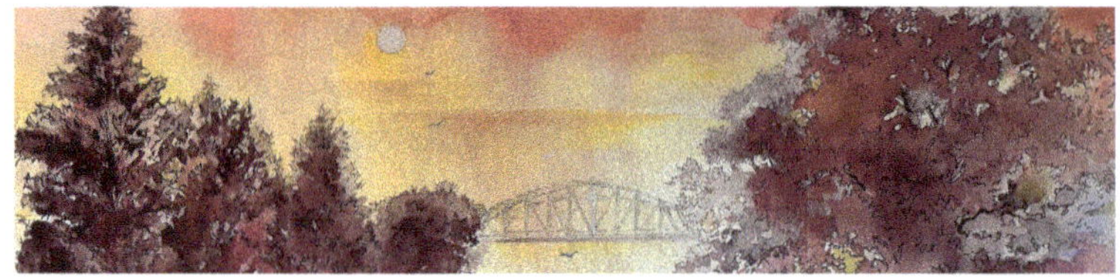

38

Passing the Baton

SARA

Tall trees frame the left side of the water-color painting, moving down the lines of perspective to the flaming horizon.

Dawn is an important theme of the painting. Night is banished, and with the first warm rays of light, the landscape of life is forever changed. Eternity beckons from a distance, offering hope for the days ahead.

Against the blush of the morning, the trees on the left represent the four children to whom the baton of faith is being passed. Their roots draw nourishment from the large parent tree on the right of the painting. Its wide branches reach upwards and its sturdy trunk grasps the earth solidly, with spreading roots that span the foreground, curling into, and around, the open Bible. Life is often brutal—its scorching seasons are only overcome by drawing from the water of the Word of God. It helped that in my reference photos of the Louisville landscape the waters of Ohio River were somewhere in that vicinity!

Jenny and Craig influenced Liz, Clara, their husbands, as well as Levi and Emma, so profoundly in the brief lives. Laura, Clara's daughter, is yet another generation to be nurtured in the wonders of a journey with God.

And there were many others, enriched by the vibrant flow of their faith, as evidenced when David had the opportunity to speak to a young audience of Jenny's high school students.

DAVID: MONDAY, AUGUST 8, 2022

Yesterday I had the privilege to speak to the high schoolers at LCA.

Jenny attended school there as she grew up and graduated in 92. She then came back to the school to work as the church secretary, teaching a class at LCA, off and on, and coaching volleyball. She was very involved in leading Bible studies with the high school girls, whom she loved dearly.

This is an excerpt of the charge that I gave these high schoolers.

"I would like to share something that I really didn't believe before Jenny died. I was unconvinced that God is interested in ALL aspects of our lives. Life was really compartmentalized for me. I had Work, Home and Church—all neatly separated. God was for Church and big needs.

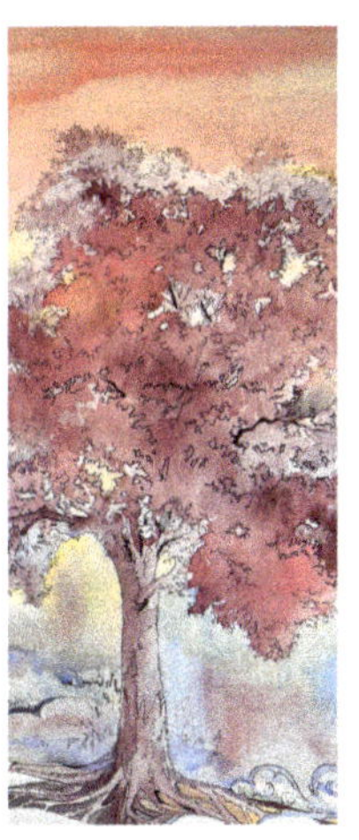

What I have come to learn is that God wants to be at the center! He belongs at the center of all aspects of life.

As I navigated my own grief as a result of Jenny's sudden death, I learned that there is great joy and unimaginable peace in the midst of grief. Each day my awe of my Great God grows—the comfort and strength He provides, hour by hour, has sustained me. All this has come as I learn to pursue Christ with my whole heart!

What does grief look like?

It really covers a broad spectrum of life experiences tinged with deep sadness—sorrow at the loss of someone we loved, or deep sorrow associated with loss of any kind. Since Jenny's death just 55 days ago, I have cried more than I ever have.

What does God say about my grief?

> *"The LORD is near*
> *to those who have*
> *a broken heart,*
> *And saves such*
> *as have a contrite spirit."*
> Psalm 34:18 NKJV
>
> *"Blessed are they that mourn:*
> *for they shall be comforted."*
> Matthew 5:4 NKJV
>
> *"The heart of the wise*
> *is in the house of mourning;*
> *but the heart of fools*
> *is in the house of mirth."*
> Ecclesiastes 7:4 NKJV

So if we are going to walk in wisdom, we are to sit in our grief. It is here that the Lord draws near to us and we should want that.

The foolish man just laughs it off, "I am fine," he says.

So if it is wise to place our hearts in the house of mourning, then we need to explore why we even have grief?

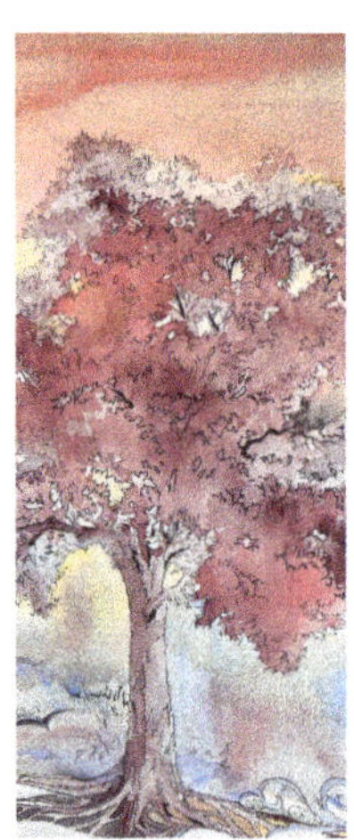

Why can't life always just be full of joy and happiness?

The answer is in a single word—sin. When sin entered the world everything changed. The serpent deceived Adam and Eve. They wanted to become like God, and the consequences that followed were ugly—pain, hard labor, and living by the sweat of our brow.

But most of all, Adam and Eve mourned the loss of the beautiful relationship they once had with their Creator. Sin brought sorrow.

Grief makes our hearts ache for God to restore what was lost —real joy! In our grieving we are reminded that this world is not meant to satisfy us.

> *"My brethren, count it all joy*
> *when you fall into various trials,*
> *knowing that the testing of your faith produces patience.*
> *But let patience have its perfect work,*
> *that you may be perfect and complete, lacking nothing."*
> James 1:2-4 NKJV

Jesus is meant to complete us. We lack nothing when we have Him.

> *"For where your treasure is,*
> *there your heart will be also."*
> Matthew 6:21 NKJV

My response to grief exposes my heart. Godly sorrow grieves deeply when we fully recognize what our great God did for us and what our sin did to Him! Godly sorrow causes us to feel crushed under the weight of our sin.

We are not just sorry briefly, only to quickly move on.

The house of mourning is not a hurried place. The verse in James mentions "patience," which is not a pit stop. We need endurance because God desires to perfect us, to grow us into His likeness. This change happens only in a heart that is wholly surrendered to Him.

Through our trial, in this house of mourning, we allow our hearts to be inspected by our great God with a true hunger and thirst for restoration. We agree with God that "the heart is deceitful and desperately wicked"—only He knows our heart. Repentance follows.

This was the posture of my heart 48 hours after Jenny's death. I realized that what I had tried to do, year after year, was to make commitments to get better—do better... I told myself that I will read more books about my God. I will do my devotions. I will read my Bible...All these things that I WILL DO.

In David's prayer in Psalm 51, there are no "I will..." statements. Instead, in his deepest repentance and yearning for forgiveness, he switches his focus to God. The Psalm is all about "YOU and YOUR.." He acknowledges His deep need! He is truly broken and he wants to deal the death blow to his sinfulness.

Have mercy upon me, O God,
According to Your lovingkindness;
According to the multitude
of Your tender mercies,
Blot out my transgressions.
Wash me thoroughly from my iniquity,
And cleanse me from my sin.
For I acknowledge my transgressions,
And my sin is always before me.
Against You, You only, have I sinned,
And done this evil in Your sight—

That You may be found just when You speak,
And blameless when You judge.
"The sacrifices of God are a broken spirit:
a broken and a contrite heart,
O God, thou wilt not despise."
Psalm 51:17 KJV

This is not a hurried process. Read the whole Psalm and notice the progression, the humble heart, bones crushed under the weight of his sin, begging, pleading, "Do YOUR work, O God!"

My truly broken heart realized that it was my sin that placed Him on the cross!

But look at what His restoration produced!

> *"Then will I teach transgressors thy ways;*
> *and sinners shall be converted unto thee."*
> Psalm 51:13 KJV

A true boldness, an eagerness to proclaim God is birthed then. David is so overwhelmed at what God has done for him that he wants this for others! He is no longer choked by sin's guilt but catches a glimpse of his purpose and destiny on earth!

As we reflect on Jenny's life here in these halls, classrooms, and on the volleyball court at LCA, what we see is a direct a result of her transformed heart.

Was she not eager to engage you to draw you to Christ?

She did her best to understand where you were, but never left you there. She compelled you to stop fearing man, but to fear God. Know Him, love Him, and grow in your knowledge of Him!

As you go into this new school year, you will best honor Jenny and glorify God, if you sit awhile in this "house of mourning." Beg God to inspect your heart, plead with Him to crush you beneath the load of your sin, so that you might see your need for Him to carry your load.

What has stolen the joy of your salvation? Who, or what, has your heart?

Lord, draw us close to you so that we may learn of your great goodness. Alert us to the lies of the devil, and this world, which pushes us to continually conform to its erroneous ways. Amen.

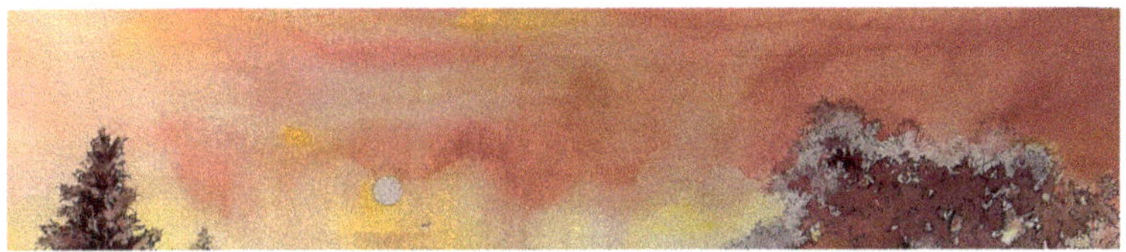

39

~※~

Next Stop: Heaven?

OR HEAVEN ON EARTH FOR YET AWHILE?

SUNDAY, AUGUST 28, 2022

Jenny....God's gift of grace to me! Your death propelled me into the arms of a loving God. It reminded me that I can't do life on my own. I need Jesus, not just when times are tough. Christ must be my all in all!

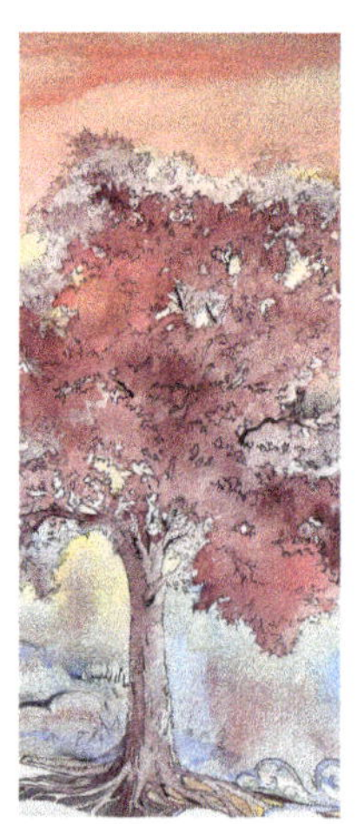

I reflect on this past week and I clearly see my grief culminating in GREAT JOY! And my heart's desire is to know Him more and to follow Him in complete obedience!

As I come to my devotional this morning, it is titled : *Guide me, Oh, thou great Jehovah.*

My pilgrim journey is hard!

God's people have always sung pilgrim songs, known as Psalms of Ascent. They contain great truths that informed a traveler's pilgrimage. The Jewish people were literally, and figuratively, ascending to worship in the city of the great King. And they were to sing these Psalms.

I am reminded that we are all pilgrims on a difficult road, through a troubled land. Our suffering can make the journey feel interminably long. And yet, we are heading up. We must keep looking up. We are traveling up to the city of the living God, the heavenly Jerusalem.

It takes supernatural effort to keep putting one weary foot in front of the other, all the while fixing our focus on our heavenly destination.

I train my heart to sing the Lord's songs in a troubled, broken land. That is how songs of faith should be sung—always with our face towards the holy city.

Oh God how great-full I am for the gift of your grace! Now my heart, mind and soul are planted firmly on the rock of my salvation. And my eyes are fixed upon you, my hope and redeemer!

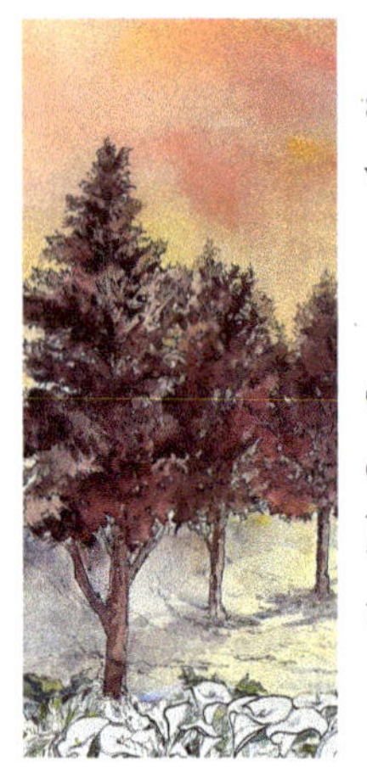

Today was our last day on the island. I started the morning capturing the sunrise, which began half way into my run!

Breakfast was at 8:30 a.m. and everyone was packed and ready to spend our last couple hours on the island, before heading back across the lake to spend the balance of the day in Mackinac City.

After breakfast, the girls and I had a very special time together on the porch of the Grand Hotel, creating our journal entry together. What a precious time! I am so thankful for my girls. Their hearts are filled with gratitude for what God is doing.

Later on the island I spent time relaxing on a park bench near the water's edge, lying on my back. My mind was flooded with memories to cherish of this week.

We traveled back across the lake on the ferry, then toured the historic Ice Breaker Boat. After an early dinner, we headed back to get our luggage at the ferry location and then on to the airport.

The airport in Pellston, Michigan, has to be the friendliest one I have ever been to! It looks nothing like a traditional airport, but more like a small ski lodge or a large log cabin, with cozy chairs and couches. We spent the next two hours playing

Shanghai, while we waited for our plane—a terrific way to end our time together, making another great memory!

Oh God, thank you so much for family and friends with whom we can share life's joys and sorrows. May we invest well in our friendships and encourage each other to know you more.

I am reminded that while I work to bring Christ's kingdom to earth, I dare not forget that my future is in another land. We must keep our eyes scanning heaven's horizon, since we'll be home soon.

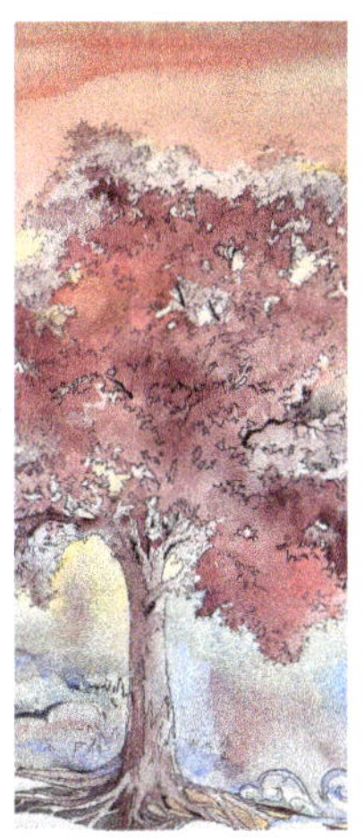

Oh God I am so very grateful for the many years you gave me with Jenny. My heart longs for the day I will see her again in eternity, as I sing your praise alongside her forevermore!

I am now at a different point in my journey.

I have spent much time contemplating how best to honor Jenny and, more importantly, my great God.

While I do not fully know how I will I do that, I feel strongly that this discipline I've built of daily reflecting on what God did for me yesterday, what I learned... has been so very helpful. It was instrumental in my spiritual growth bringing me through my grieving.

So I will continue to do it. It just will not be purposefully written to only remember Jenny, but rather to focus more on getting to know God.

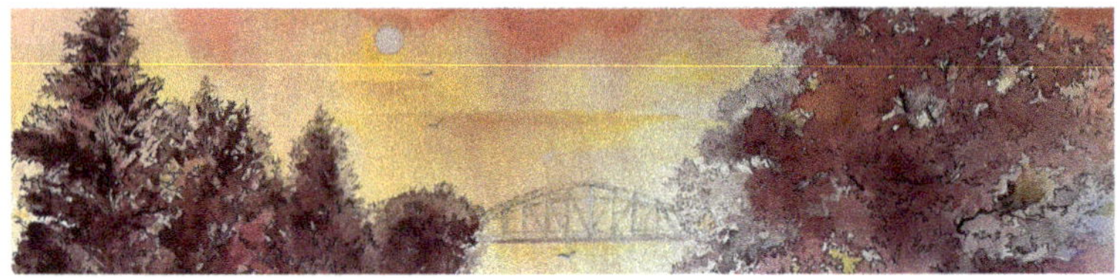

40

David's Proposal to Rachel

Rachel, my heart is so filled with joy and gratitude as in you I see God's grace extended to me. What a great God we serve, the Giver of all good gifts—the gift of your heart! I marvel that He would entrust you to me.

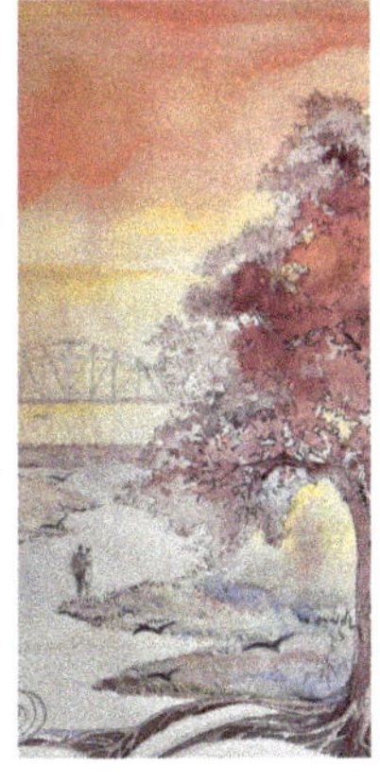

I now ask you to join me on the road of grace and run beside me toward the dawn. I would treasure the opportunity to share this life alongside you. It's a narrow road and the race will be hard.

In Hebrews, God calls for us to run this race with perseverance (difficulty—delay in achieving success.)

> *Wherefore seeing we also*
> *are compassed about*
> *with so great a cloud of witnesses,*
> *let us lay aside every weight,*
> *and the sin which doth so easily beset us,*
> *and let us run with patience*
> *the race that is set before us,*
> *Looking unto Jesus…*
> Hebrews 12:1

His grace went through me like a sword.

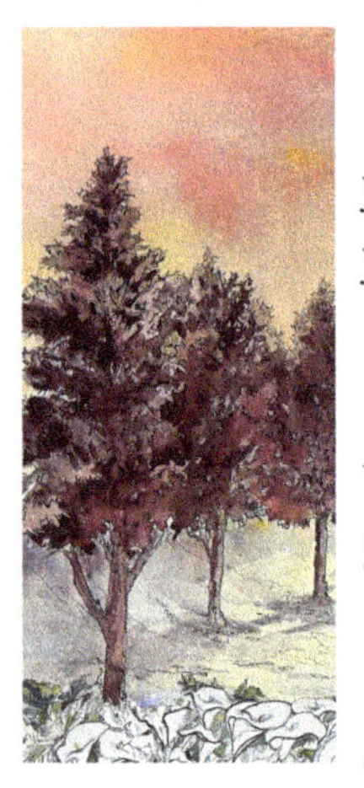

Rachel, God's grace was on display in your life when you shared how He had kept you, as you navigated Craig's sudden death.

You encouraged me in the midst of the valley that I was now entering—and His grace was wielded like a sword.

His very words brought life, propelled me out into the light to come out finally like a song. He has placed that song in my heart and opened my mouth to declare His praise.

I now ask you to join me on this road of grace—to run

beside me—running toward the dawn—toiling in the shadows of the dawn, that our great God might be glorified in our lives.

Rachel, I need you!
I need you to love Christ and seek His face. I need you to rest in Him!

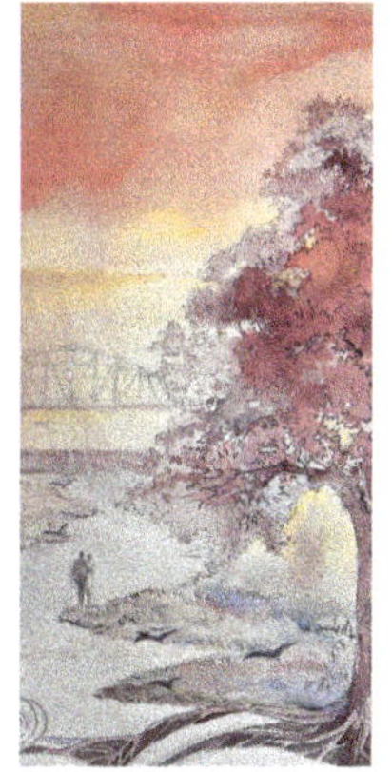

I need your words of affirmation. I need your respect. I need you to partner closely with me to help me slow down and consider how my quickness to act may hurt others.

I need your companionship.

I need your encouragement. I love how you fan the flames of my heart, encouraging, and promoting my growth in godliness.

I need your honesty. I treasure your heart's ready willingness to be guided by me, while wholly trusting in our great God.

Rachel... will you marry me?

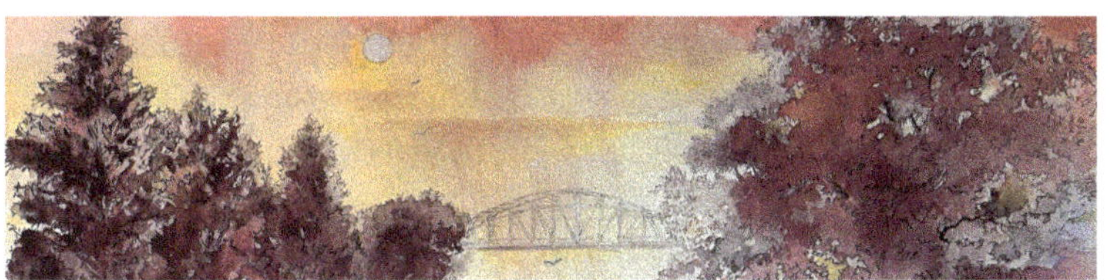

4I

After the Last Brushstroke

SARA

I roll up the painting carefully and tie it with a cheery red ribbon. I make the short drive over later in the day to my local UPS store to have it packed and shipped.

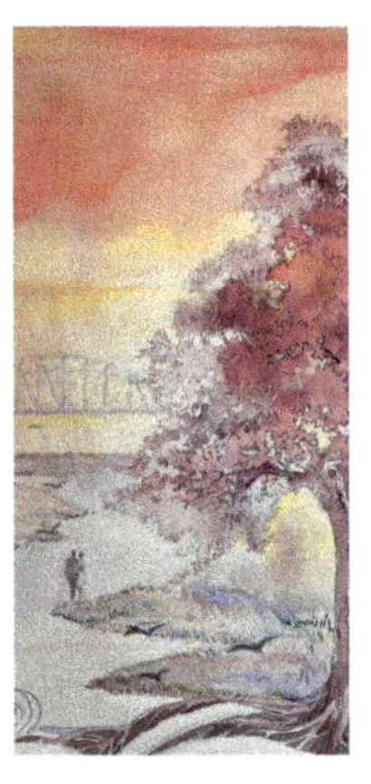

It is a quiet afternoon and the store is mostly empty, except for one sleepy young man behind the desk. He cushions the painting carefully in a box, walks me through the process of insuring it, and finally sends it on its way to its intended home.

My studio is a mess! When I work, I lose myself in the

process. Shipping this work was at a far more relaxed pace than when I had to send David the digital image for his proposal.

Now engaged, they are busy planning a spring wedding in March. While waiting eagerly for the painting to arrive, they called me excitedly. Another happy call came when it finally reached them. It was then off to the framers with discussions on where it might hang in their new home. Their joy was my joy!

The hope of years together stretches ahead of them—as many as the Lord will bless them with. They have their merged families and innumerable friends who are delighted to celebrate their union. Life beckons with its potential for more adventures in their shared mission.

They faced death and came out victorious, knowing well that without Jesus they could be hopeless, bitter or angry, instead of filled with excitement about the future! Joy infuses their lives now—a greater blessing than mere happiness.

Wedding plans crowded out any further conversations with them. In agreement with their desire to inspire others to love their "great God" as deeply as they did, I prayed for their efforts.

The sun will rise again for each of us to-morrow, bringing us another day of opportunity to cherish.

With whom will we each share Jesus?

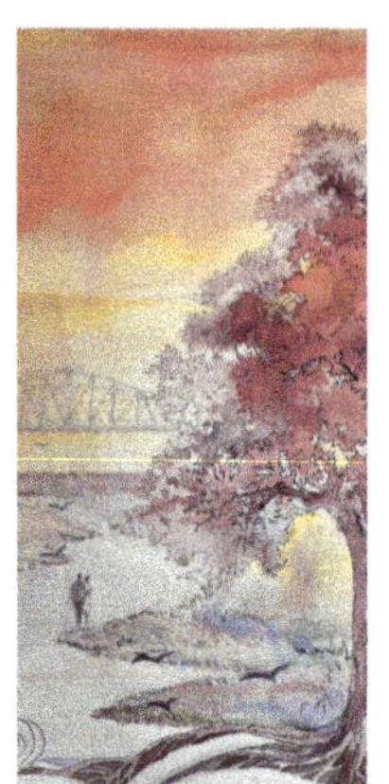

I will pick up my brushes, stretch paper and dream about what to paint next with His help.

David and Rachel will tell someone who is hurting that He can heal all wounds and broken hearts.

Our actions are motivated by the hope that someone will be touched by our labors in our service to Jesus.

Our means are different, yet our mission is the same—to love Jesus and to make Him known.

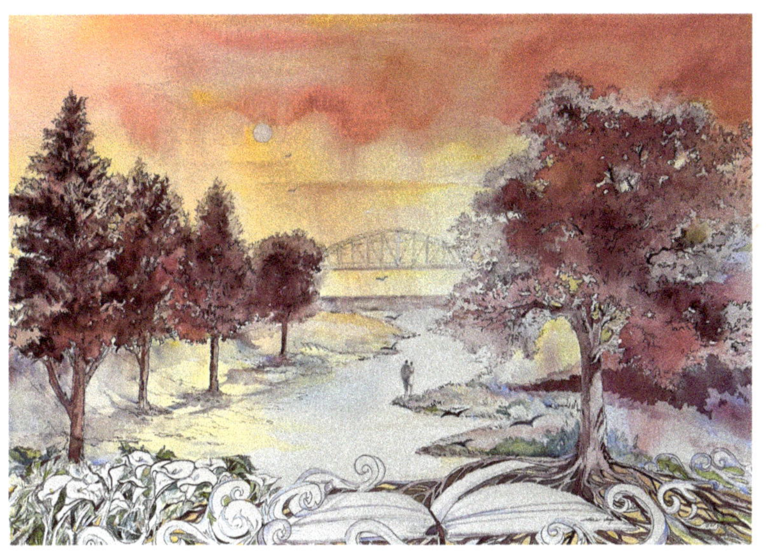

Grace
Sara Joseph

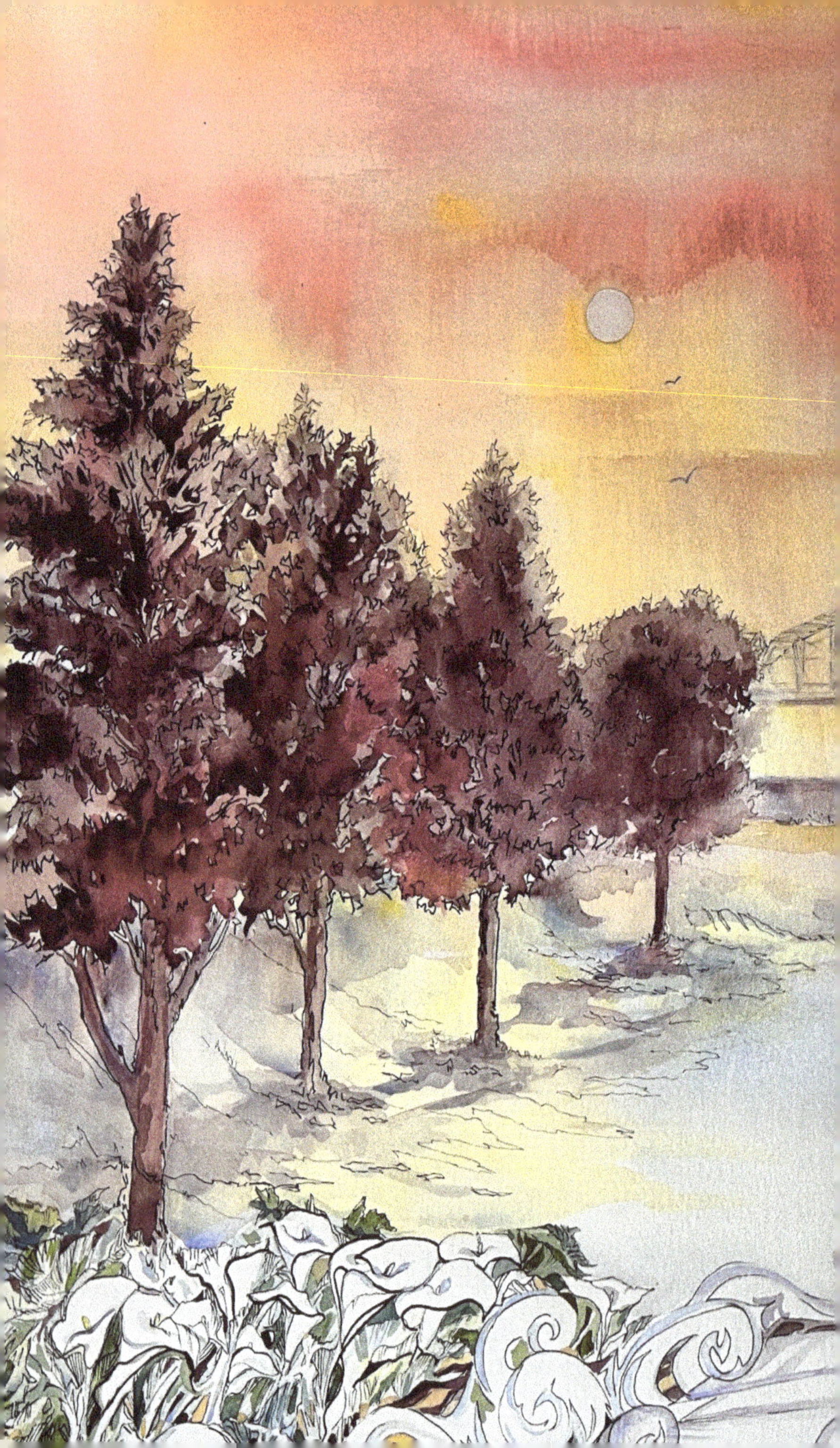

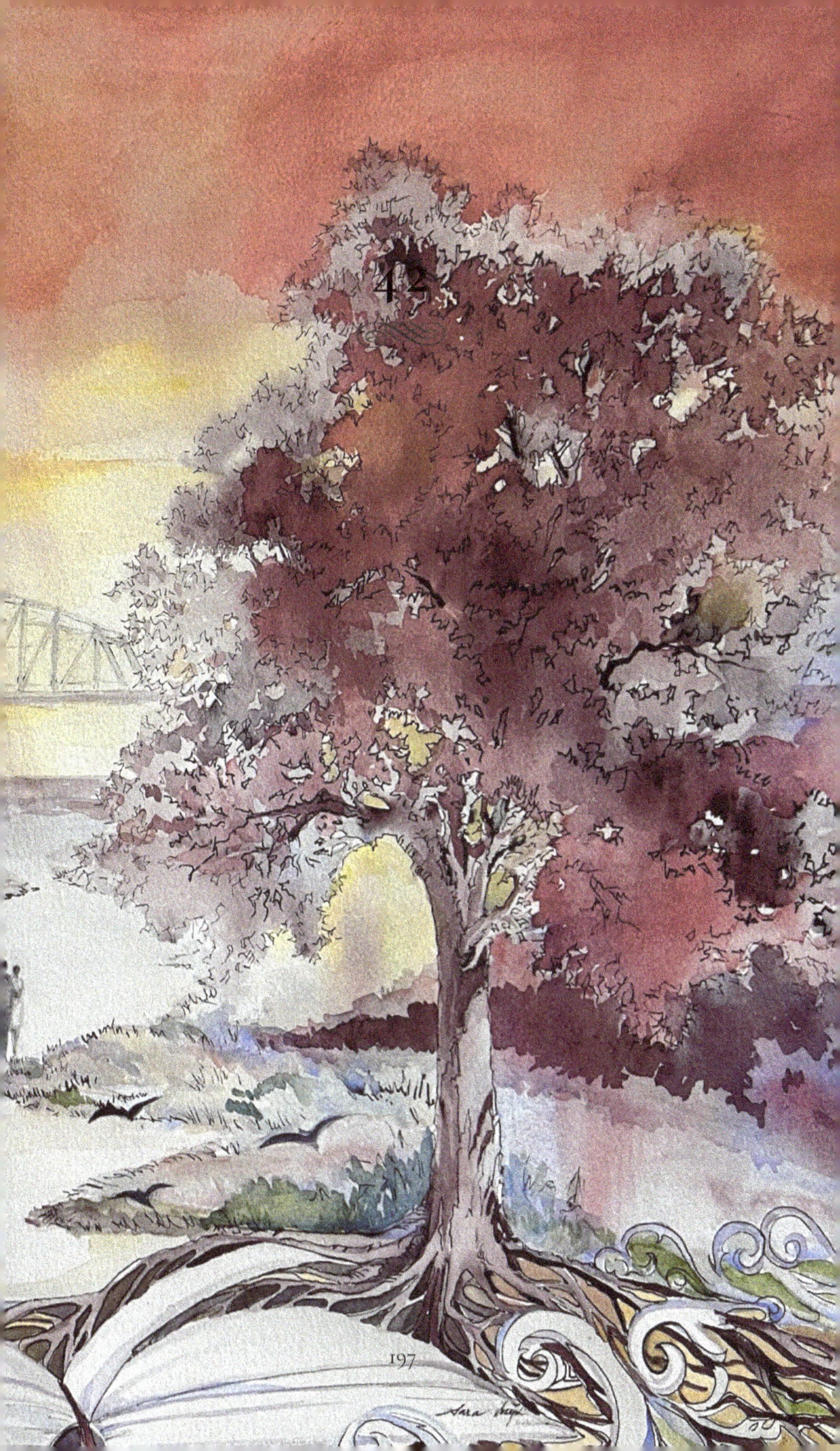
42

As a Christian artist who paints in watercolors, acrylics, oils, inks and mixed media, I've been undeservedly fortunate. The Lord blessed the artwork of my hands to be in numerous private and corporate collections around the world—a privilege I never imagined when I first wet my brush and loaded it with color.

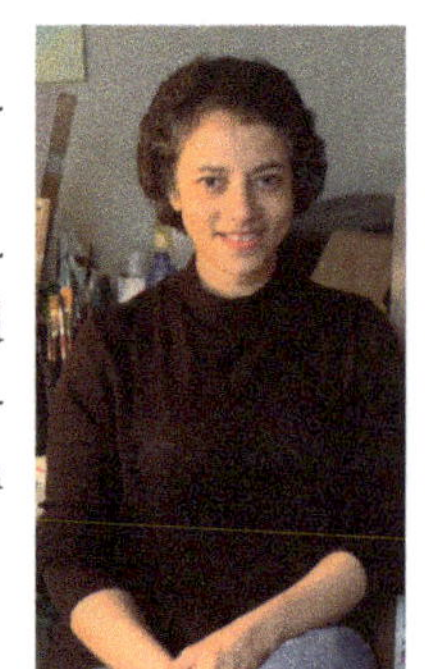

As a sculptor, I've enjoyed many happy years studying figurative sculpture with live models, working in stoneware and terracotta. I now prefer to sculpt in colorful polymer clays. Together with other artists, I co-owned a gallery in Dallas for about a decade—an adventure I doubt I'd want to relive, despite its many joys!

Teaching Bible classes in my home church is a blessing that keeps my relationship with Jesus fresh and exciting. I am currently on another unexpected twist in my journey engaging younger artists in visual exploration by sharing my delight in art and its creative processes.

All the good in my life is because of Jesus. I'm more passionate about Him than writing, art, design or creativity. I enjoy expressing visual praise to God for a redeemed, beautiful life.

Commission Art

Let me capture the beauty of your story. I'd love to work with you, as I did with David and Rachel to help you manifest your dream, idea or aspiration in an original work of art to cherish for a lifetime!

OTHER BOOKS BY SARA JOSEPH

- Gently Awakened: The Influence of Faith on Your Artistic Journey
- Consider the Lilies: An Adult Coloring Devotional Journal
- The Power of the Seed: An Adult Coloring Devotional Journal

AUTHOR WEBSITE: SARAJOSEPH.ART

LinkedIn: https://www.linkedin.com/in/sjoseph
Instagram: https://www.instagram.com/sara_and_art/
Pinterest: https://www.pinterest.com/artsarajoseph/